Science Directions

CO-ORDINATOR'S HANDBOOK

Chris Sunley
Jane Bourne
Alison Norman

COLLINS

Published by HarperCollins*Publishers* Limited
77–85 Fulham Palace Road
Hammersmith
London
W6 8JB

www.CollinsEducation.com
On-line support for schools and colleges

ISBN 0 00 317 2570

Based on a scheme of work known as *Science 3–11* developed
and provided by Suffolk County Council.

Chris Sunley, Alison Norman and Jane Bourne assert the
moral right to be identified as the authors of this work.

British Library Cataloguing in Publication Data.
A catalogue record for this publication is available from the
British Library.

Design and production by Perry Tate Design

Illustrations by Sami Sweeten and Phil Burrows
Cover photographs by: Stone/Myron; Images Colour Library;
Stone/Renee Lynn; Allsport UK/Clive Mason; Telegraph
Colour Library/NASA; Premium/Robert Harding
Picture Library.

You might also like to visit
www.**fire**and**water**.com
The book lover's website

Printed by Martins, Berwick

Contents

What is Science Directions?

Science Directions is a comprehensive and detailed scheme of work for pupils aged 3–11. It complies fully with the requirements of the Foundation Stage as specified in Early Learning Goals, and with the Science National Curriculum programmes of study for Key Stages 1 and 2. Science Directions is also matched to the exemplar schemes of work produced by the Qualifications and Curriculum Authority (QCA). Moreover, the time allocations and titles of the Science Directions units mirror those in the QCA scheme of work.

Science Directions is based on a successful scheme entitled *Science 3—11*, which was produced by teachers and advisory staff in Suffolk LEA and completed in 1995. It has been used extensively in the county and more widely in other parts of the country since 1995. The key feature and central aim of *Science 3—11* is to support a cyclical approach to the development of skills, knowledge and understanding through the careful choice of activities and context. This approach has been refined and further developed in Science Directions. Ideas are revisited to consolidate and extend pupils' understanding through carefully chosen activities that eliminate unnecessary duplication of work undertaken in earlier years. Many of the other features of *Science 3—11* have been retained and the content fully updated to meet the current programme of study requirements.

Science Directions has a straightforward structure. The Early Years material comprises a Teaching File, a Big Book and a set of six Story Books. These provide careful guidance and resources to enable teachers to plan and organise high-quality activities. Material for Years 1 to 6 comprises one Teaching File and one Pupil Book for each school year. For each unit of work, the Teaching File provides detailed teachers' notes covering a range of activities. Many of the activities are drawn from the QCA schemes of work; others are new, and extend the range of experiences for pupils.

What Are the Aims of Science Directions?

The aims can be summarised as follows:

For Pupils

- to provide a rich and stimulating scientific experience that will foster a fascination and interest in science;
- to present science as an essentially practical experience based largely on first-hand experiences in relevant contexts;
- to develop investigative approaches to scientific enquiry that build the confidence necessary to tackle problems with increasing levels of independence;
- to encourage discussion of scientific ideas, and the abilities to question and to justify;
- to support a sense of scientific curiosity, and the development of appropriate levels of knowledge and understanding.

For Teachers

- to provide an accessible framework of advice and information, which closely integrates teacher and pupil material;
- to link the National Curriculum programmes of study to appropriate and interesting activities with a range of possible pupil outcomes;
- to support continuity and progression in learning between different years and key stages, and encourage a constructivist approach in which new ideas are developed from existing ones;
- to encourage the use of questioning to clarify, consolidate and extend understanding;
- to provide explicit links between the activities and support materials and National Curriculum levels of attainment, so that assessment of pupil progress can be ongoing and informative;
- to support teachers by providing background information on the underlying scientific ideas and principles being developed.

How Does Science Directions Match the Early Learning Goals?

Early Learning Goals towards Knowledge and Understanding of the World

The scientific focus of Science Directions enables children to be working towards the early learning goals described as **knowledge and understanding of the world**.

In this area of learning, children are developing the skills, knowledge and understanding that help them to make sense of the world. This forms the foundation for later work in science, history, geography, design and technology, and information and communication technology.

By the end of the foundation stage, most children will be able to:

K1 investigate objects and materials by using all of their senses as appropriate;

K2 find out about, and identify some features of, living things, objects and events they observe;

K3 look closely at similarities, differences, patterns and change;

K4 ask questions about why things happen and how things work;

K5 build and construct with a wide range of objects, selecting appropriate resources, and adapting their work where necessary;

K6 select the tools and techniques they need to shape, assemble and join the materials they are using;

K7 find out about and identify the uses of everyday technology and use information and communication technology, and programmable toys, to support their learning;

K8 find out about past and present events in their own lives, and in those of their families and other people they know;

K9 observe, find out about and identify features in the place they live and in the natural world;

K10 begin to know about their own cultures and beliefs, and those of other people;

K11 find out about their environment, and talk about those features they like and dislike.

Science Directions	Early Learning Goals										
	K1	K2	K3	K4	K5	K6	K7	K8	K9	K10	K11
Working Out of Doors											
Special Places									•		•
Treasure Hunt		•							•		•
A Pot of Plants		•									
Looking for Leaves		•	•								
Small Animal Search		•	•								
Making Habitats		•							•		
Seasonal Activities											
Muddy Puddles	•	•	•	•							
Shadow Play	•	•	•	•							
Feeding the Birds		•	•								
Streamers and Bubbles	•	•		•							
Autumn Faces	•	•	•		•						
Ice Cold Animals	•	•	•								

Science Directions	Early Learning Goals										
	K1	K2	K3	K4	K5	K6	K7	K8	K9	K10	K11
Looking at Ourselves											
Looking in the Mirror	●	●									
Scarecrows	●	●									
Hairy Puppets	●	●	●								
Hand Built	●		●	●	●						
Smelly Cards	●										
I Packed my Bag								●		●	
Making Special Places											
In the Dark Cave	●	●	●	●			●				
The Shoe Shop	●	●	●	●				●			
The Garden Centre	●	●	●								
The Recycling Centre	●		●		●	●					
Sand Play											
Burrowing	●		●	●	●						
Sand Castles	●		●	●	●						
Trickling Sand	●		●	●		●					
Falling Cliffs	●		●	●							
Buried Treasure	●	●	●	●		●					
Helter-Skelter	●	●	●	●	●						
Water Play											
Moving Water		●	●	●							
Drops and Streams		●		●		●					
Drip Drop	●	●	●	●		●					
Squeezing and Squirting		●	●	●		●					
Fill It Up		●	●	●		●					
Putting Them in Water	●		●	●							
Cooking and Food											
Fruit Salad	●	●	●								
Banana Bread	●		●			●					
Fruity Drinks	●		●			●					
A Big Breakfast	●		●								
One Potato, Two Potato	●	●	●								
Bread Roll Faces	●				●						
Art Activities											
Mixing and Painting	●		●	●		●					
Sponge Splat!	●		●								
Drippy Pictures	●		●			●					
Playing with Dough	●		●		●	●					
Sticking Pictures	●		●		●						
Making Coloured Windows	●	●									
Sound and Listening											
Making Sounds	●		●								
Making Shakers	●		●		●						
Musical Kim's Game		●	●								
The Echo		●	●	●							
A Listening Walk							●		●		●
Telephones		●	●				●				
Toys and Games											
Playing Skittles		●		●							
Toys That Move		●	●	●				●			
Rolling Along		●	●	●	●	●					
Playing with Balloons		●	●	●							
A Magnet Show	●	●		●	●						
Up in the Air		●		●	●		●				

How Does Science Directions Match the Programmes of Study for Key Stages 1 and 2?

		The Programme of Study References Covered in Each Unit			
YEAR	UNIT TITLE	**Sc1*** Scientific enquiry	**Sc2** Life processes and living things	**Sc3** Materials and their properties	**Sc4** Physical processes
1	Ourselves, 1A	2c, 2f, 2h, 2j	1a, 1b, 2a, 2g, 4a		
1	Growing Plants, 1B	2c, 2f, 2g, 2h, 2j	1b, 2a, 2b, 2c, 2e, 3a, 3b, 5b, 5c		
1	Sorting and Using Materials, 1C	2c, 2d, 2f, 2i, 2j		1a, 1b, 1c, 1d	
1	Light and Dark, 1D	2c, 2g, 2h	2g		3a, 3b
1	Pushes and Pulls, 1E	2c, 2f, 2g, 2h, 2i, 2j			2a, 2b, 2c
1	Sound and Hearing, 1F	2c, 2d, 2f, 2i, 2j	2g		3c, 3d
2	Health and Growth, 2A	2c, 2f, 2h, 2j	2b, 2f, 2g		
2	Plants and Animals in the Local Environment, 2B	2c, 2g, 2h, 2j	2f, 3c, 5b, 5c		
2	Variation, 2C	2c, 2d, 2f, 2g, 2h	1a, 2e, 4a, 4b, 5b		
2	Grouping and Changing Materials, 2D	2c, 2f, 2h, 2i		1c, 1d, 2a, 2b	
2	Forces and Movement, 2E	2c, 2d, 2f, 2h, 2i		2a	2a, 2b, 2c
2	Using Electricity, 2F	2e			1a, 1b, 1c
3	Teeth and Eating, 3A	2c, 2d, 2f, 2i, 2j	1a, 2a, 2b		
3	Helping Plants Grow Well, 3B	2c, 2f, 2i, 2j	1b, 2b, 3a, 3b, 3c		
3	Characteristics of Materials, 3C	2c, 2d, 2f, 2h, 2i, 2j, 2l		1a	
3	Rocks and Soils, 3D	2c, 2d, 2f, 2i, 2k, 2l		1a, 1d, 3a	
3	Magnets and Springs, 3E	2c, 2d, 2f, 2i, 2j, 2l			2a, 2b, 2e
3	Light and Shadows, 3F	2c, 2f, 2i, 2m			3a, 3b, 4b
4	Moving and Growing, 4A	2c, 2f, 2i, 2m	1a, 2c, 2e		
4	Habitats, 4B	2c, 2d, 2f, 2i	1c, 4a, 4b, 5a, 5b, 5c, 5d, 5e		

* Programmes of study elements 2a, 2b and 2e are implicit in the work of all units.

		The Programme of Study References Covered in Each Unit			
		Sc1*	Sc2	Sc3	Sc4
YEAR	UNIT TITLE	Scientific enquiry	Life processes and living things	Materials and their properties	Physical processes
4	Keeping Warm, 4C	2c, 2d, 2f, 2i, 2k, 2l		1a, 1b, 1c, 2c	
4	Solids and Liquids, 4D	2c, 2d, 2f, 2h, 2j, 2k, 2m		1a, 2a, 2d, 2f, 3a, 3b, 3c, 3e	
4	Friction, 4E	2c, 2f, 2g, 2j, 2k, 2l			2c, 2e
4	Circuits and Conductors, 4F	2c, 2f, 2h, 2i, 2j, 2k, 2l		1c	1a, 1b
5	Keeping Healthy, 5A	2c, 2f, 2i, 2j	1a, 2b, 2c, 2d, 2e, 2g, 2h		
5	Life Cycles, 5B	2c, 2d, 2f, 2g, 2i, 2j	1a, 1b, 2f, 3a, 3d		
5	Gases All Around, 5C	2c, 2d, 2f, 2h, 2j, 2l, 2m		1a, 1e, 2b	2c
5	Changing State, 5D	2c, 2f, 2g, 2i, 2j, 2m		1e, 2c, 2d, 2e	
5	Earth, Sun and Moon, 5E	2c, 2d, 2f, 2g, 2h, 2i, 2j, 2m			4a, 4b, 4c, 4d
5	Sound All Around, 5F	2c, 2f, 2g, 2h, 2i, 2j			3e, 3f, 3g
6	Interdependence and Adaptation, 6A	2c, 2f, 2i, 2j	1b, 1c, 3a, 3b, 3c, 4a, 5b, 5c, 5d, 5e		
6	Micro-organisms (short unit), 6B	2c, 2d, 2f, 2g, 2h, 2i, 2j, 2m	2b, 2f, 5f		
6	More About Dissolving, 6C	2c, 2d, 2f, 2g, 2i, 2j, 2l		3a, 3b, 3c, 3d	
6	Reversible and Irreversible Changes (short unit), 6D	2c, 2d, 2f, 2g, 2h, 2i, 2l, 2m		2a, 2b, 2f, 2g, 3c, 3d	
6	Forces in Action, 6E	2c, 2d, 2f, 2g, 2i, 2l, 2m			2b, 2c, 2d, 2e
6	How We See Things (short unit), 6F	2c, 2h, 2i, 2j, 2m			3a, 3c, 3d
6	Changing Circuits (short unit), 6G	2c, 2f, 2h, 2i, 2j, 2l, 2m			1a, 1b, 1c

* Programmes of study elements 2a, 2b and 2e are implicit in the work of all units.

How Are the Early Years Materials Organised?

Using the First Page of Each Unit

The first page of each unit provides general information about organisation and resources.

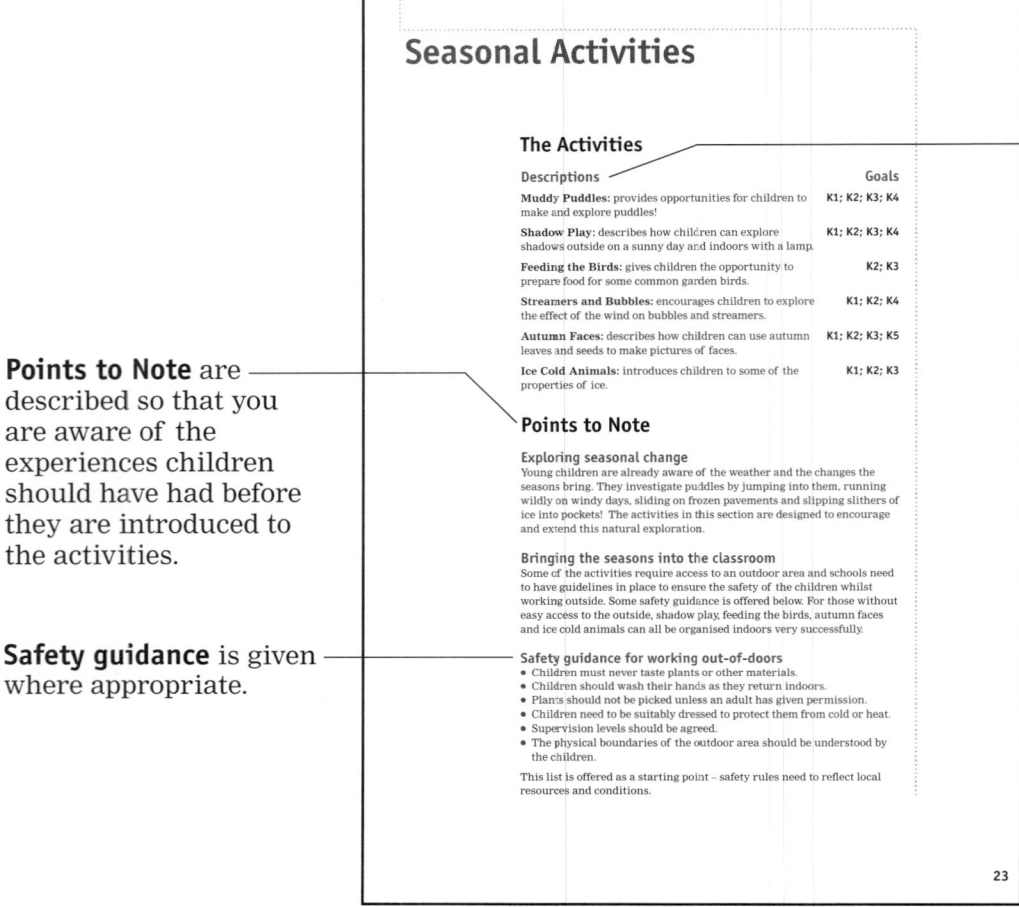

Points to Note are described so that you are aware of the experiences children should have had before they are introduced to the activities.

Safety guidance is given where appropriate.

A brief description is given of each activity in the unit so that you can see at a glance the skills and knowledge contained in it. The numerical code next to the descriptions indicates which **early learning goals** the children will be working towards during the activity. The early learning goals identified in this section all relate to knowledge and understanding of the world. *For example, K9 shows that children will 'observe, find out about and identify features in the place they live and the natural world'.*

A grid showing the match between the activities and early learning goals is given on pages 6–7 of this Handbook.

Other goals related to personal, social and emotional development, and linguistic skills, will also be a feature of each activity but have not been separately identified here.

Using the Teaching Activities

Skills

This section identifies the scientific skills that children will be developing during the activity.

Vocabulary

This shows some of the vocabulary that can be developed during the activity. Some of the words may be new to the children and by using them in context you can encourage language development.

Resources

This lists equipment needed for the activity. Advice on where to collect resources and how to make some equipment is also included.

Points to Note

This gives additional pointers for success and other organisational suggestions.

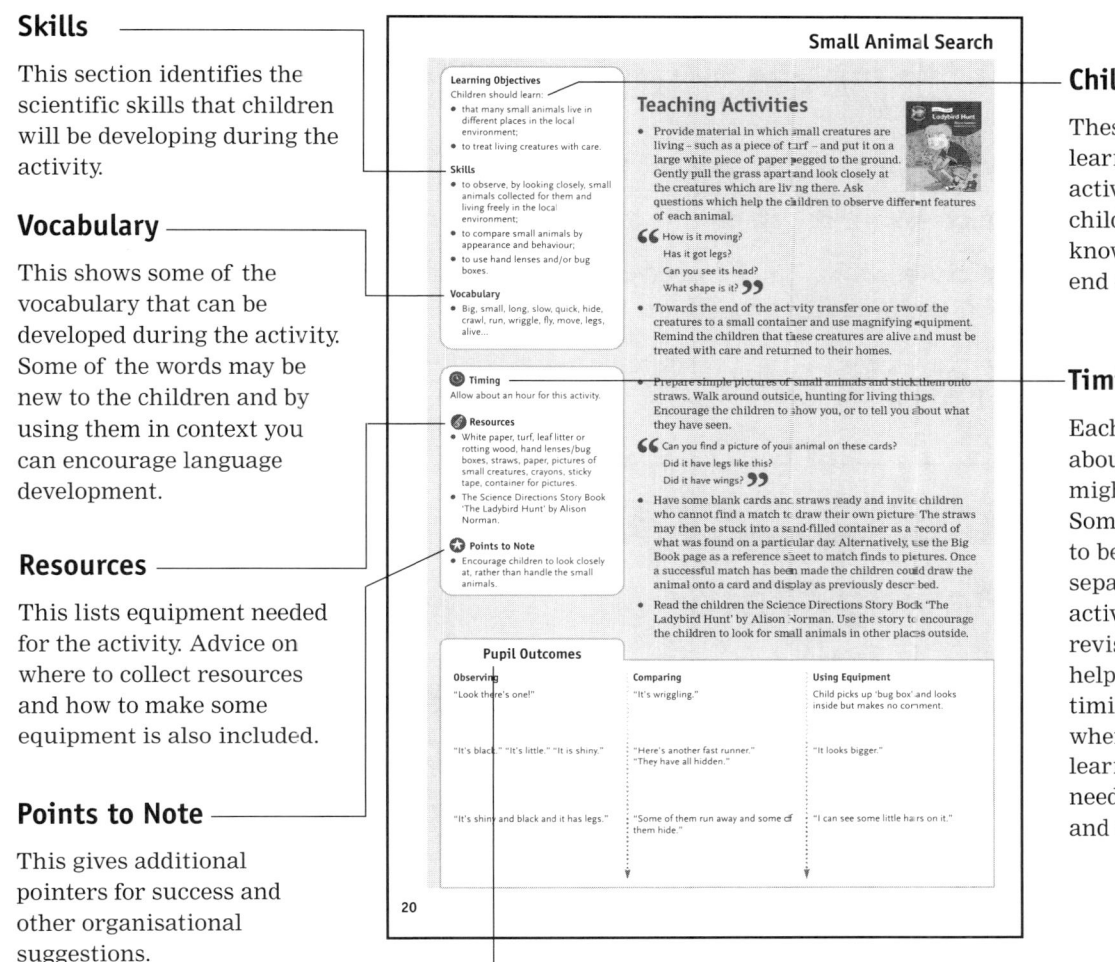

Children should learn

These statements are the learning objectives for the activity. They describe what children might be expected to know or understand by the end of the activity.

Timing

Each page includes guidance about the time an activity might be expected to take. Some activities are designed to be organised into several separate parts. Other activities are designed to be revisited. The guidance offers help on these issues. The timings are only a guide; when young children have learnt something new, they need the freedom to repeat and explore it through play.

Pupil Outcomes and Assessment

The possible pupil outcomes for an activity are shown in tabular form at the bottom of each page. They provide indicators of learning and progression in seven specific scientific skills: Observing; Comparing; Communicating; Sorting; Grouping; Measuring; Making Guesses; Using New Equipment.

Safety

The safety symbol shows when there are health and safety issues to be considered.

Story Book Links

Some activities are supported by a Story Book. Story Books can provide a starting point for, or an extension to, the children's practical experiences.

The Activity Description

This section describes how each activity can be introduced and organised. In addition, there are suggestions for open-ended questions. These will help you to guide and extend the children's exploration and to develop their language. The material provides opportunities for children to work alone and in large and small groups.

The Big Book

The Science Directions Big Book is designed as a resource to support and extend the activities in the Early Years Teaching File.

The Book:

provides a resource for use with large or small groups;

stimulates discussion between an adult and a child as well as between groups of children;

encourages children to observe and compare;

provides pictures which can give a starting point for practical activities;

provides pictures which can be used to extend the ideas that children have met in the practical activities;

provides pictures which are a resource linking the children's activities to wider applications.

WATER PLAY

Moving Water

- These pictures all show moving water. What can you see?

19

The Story Books

The Science Directions Story Books are linked to ideas about materials, forces and living things. They have been written to capture the imagination of the children through strong narrative and appealing characters. The stories have settings that will be familiar to young children, and contain a small surprise so that children can imagine themselves in the story and be entertained by the turn of events.

Each story is supported by two levels of text. The large text carries the story whilst the smaller text supports and extends this story by introducing new ideas.

The Story Books can be directly linked to specific activities in the Teaching File and, where this is the case, the activity description shows a picture of the cover of the appropriate story.

We stamped in the puddle and made splashes on the fence.

splosh

bang

If the children stamp really hard they can make the water splash a long way.

8

The water is hitting the fence.

splash

Who is getting wet?

9

How Are the Teaching Files for Years 1–6 Organised?

The teaching file includes:

- teaching activities with detailed explanations for each unit;
- a set of photocopiable masters for each unit.

Each unit is set out in the following way:

Introductory page of the Unit

Timing

Approximate time needed for teaching the unit, based on the recommendations in the QCA scheme of work.

Glossary of terms

Clear explanations for teachers of key scientific terms relevant to the unit.

Starting points

Ideas that pupils will have encountered through earlier work with Science Directions.

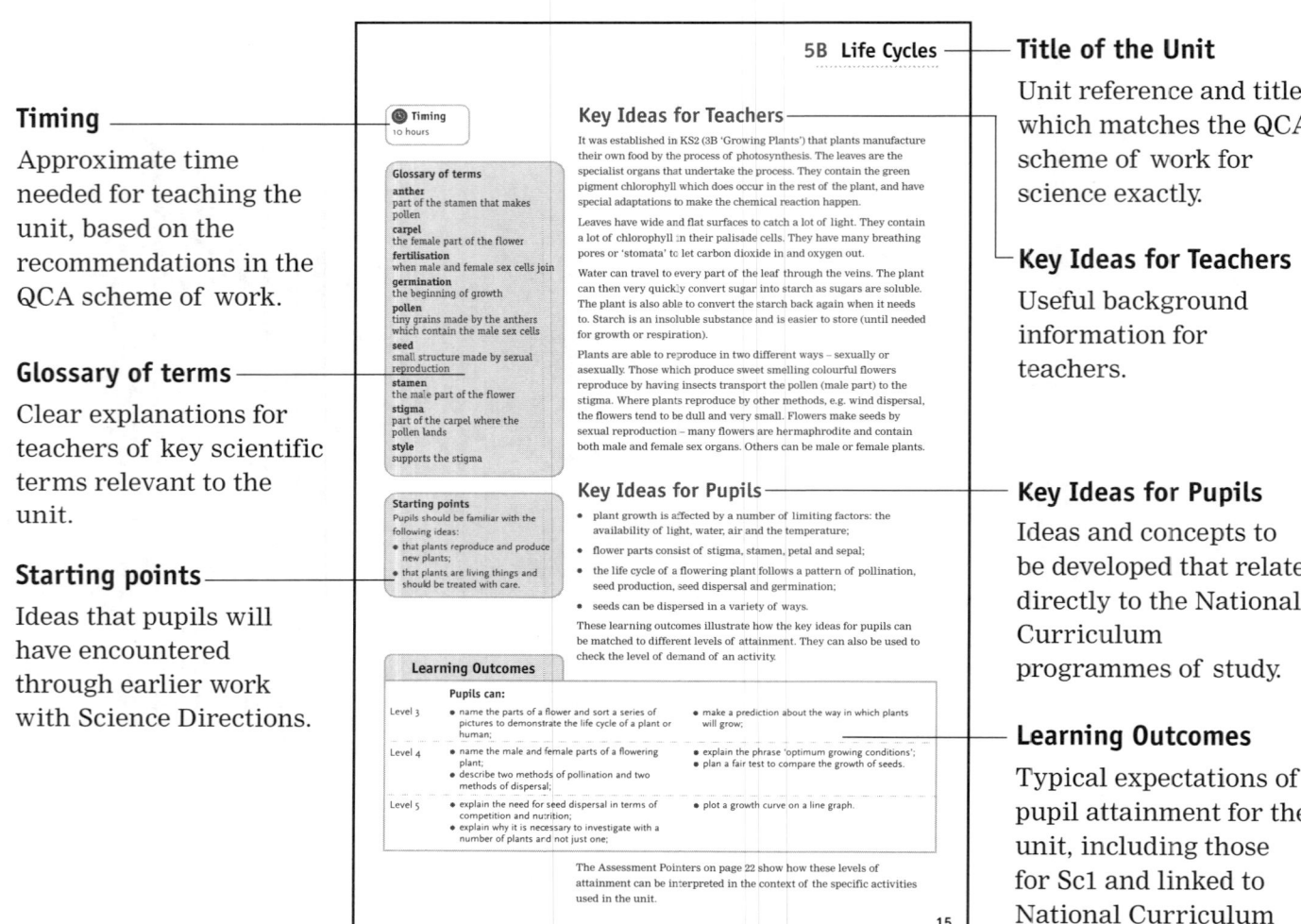

Title of the Unit

Unit reference and title, which matches the QCA scheme of work for science exactly.

Key Ideas for Teachers

Useful background information for teachers.

Key Ideas for Pupils

Ideas and concepts to be developed that relate directly to the National Curriculum programmes of study.

Learning Outcomes

Typical expectations of pupil attainment for the unit, including those for Sc1 and linked to National Curriculum levels.

Unit Activities

Timing

Approximate time to cover the activities.

Resources

Summary of resources needed and the key words that pupils should be introduced to during the activities.

Safety

Safety issues specific to the activities. Teachers should always make a risk assessment for the particular group of pupils they are teaching.

Pupil materials

Reference to photocopiable masters and pages in the Pupil's Book that relate directly to these activities. A summary of each photocopiable master and pupil page is given to aid clarity.

Key Activity

An activity that allows pupils to demonstrate their knowledge, skills and understanding of the unit. This is usually the final activity in the unit. In almost all cases, it provides a specific opportunity to develop and practise Sc1 investigative skills. If required, the activity can also be used to assess pupils' progress in Sc1.

Teaching Activities

Detailed guidance on how to organise and sequence the various activities. Particular emphasis is given to the questions that challenge pupils' thinking and ideas.

Pupil Consolidation

Suggestions of other tasks and activities that the pupils can be given to consolidate their learning. In many cases the activities will tend to broaden and extend understanding. As such, they are more likely to be used with selected groups of pupils rather than with the whole class.

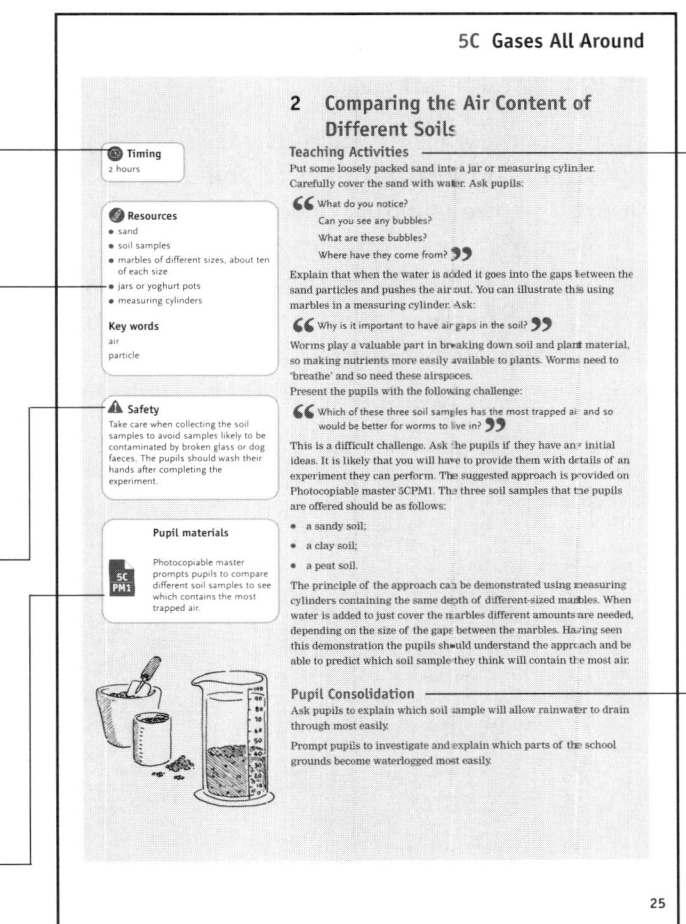

End-of-Unit Assessment

Assessment Pointers for Sc1

Possible learning outcomes for the Key Activity are provided, as well as some of those given on the first page of the unit. To simplify the assessment process, the learning outcomes are arranged under the 'strands' of 'planning', 'obtaining and presenting evidence', and 'considering evidence and evaluating'. The outcomes have been written to relate directly to the particular context of the Key Activity and include the type of response expected at each level of attainment. They are not exhaustive and so there will be many other acceptable responses.

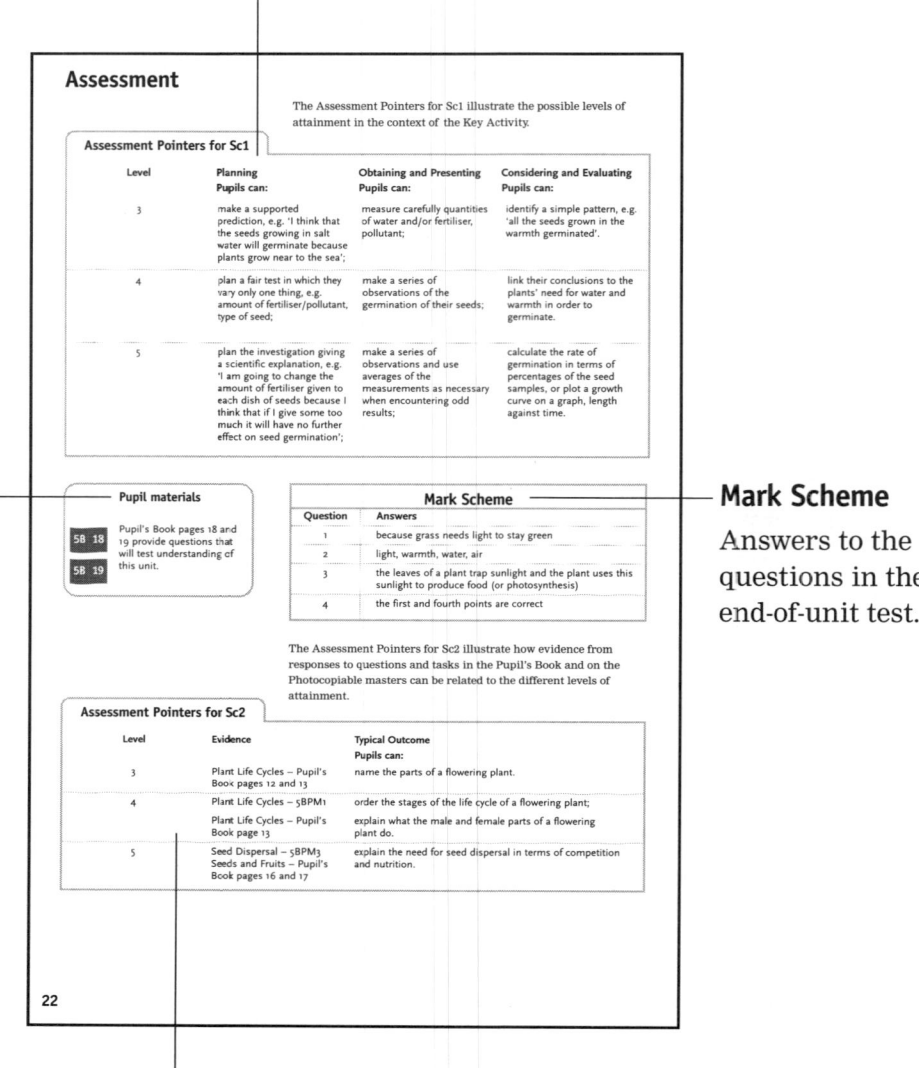

Pupil materials

Reference to one of the photocopiable masters, which can be used as an end-of-unit test.

Mark Scheme

Answers to the questions in the end-of-unit test.

Assessment Pointers for the Appropriate Knowledge-based Attainment Target, i.e. Sc2, 3 or 4

Indicators of attainment related to the learning outcomes given at the beginning of the unit, placed in the context of questions from the Pupil Book and photocopiable masters. Thus, by looking back through the pupil's work, it should be possible to match the work to an overall level of attainment for the unit.

How Are the Pupil Books for Years 1–6 Organised?

Drawings and Photographs

Illustrations are used extensively, not only to convey information, but also to stimulate interest and illustrate the relevance of the scientific ideas being considered.

They should provide a stimulus for discussion and questioning, both with individuals and the class as a whole.

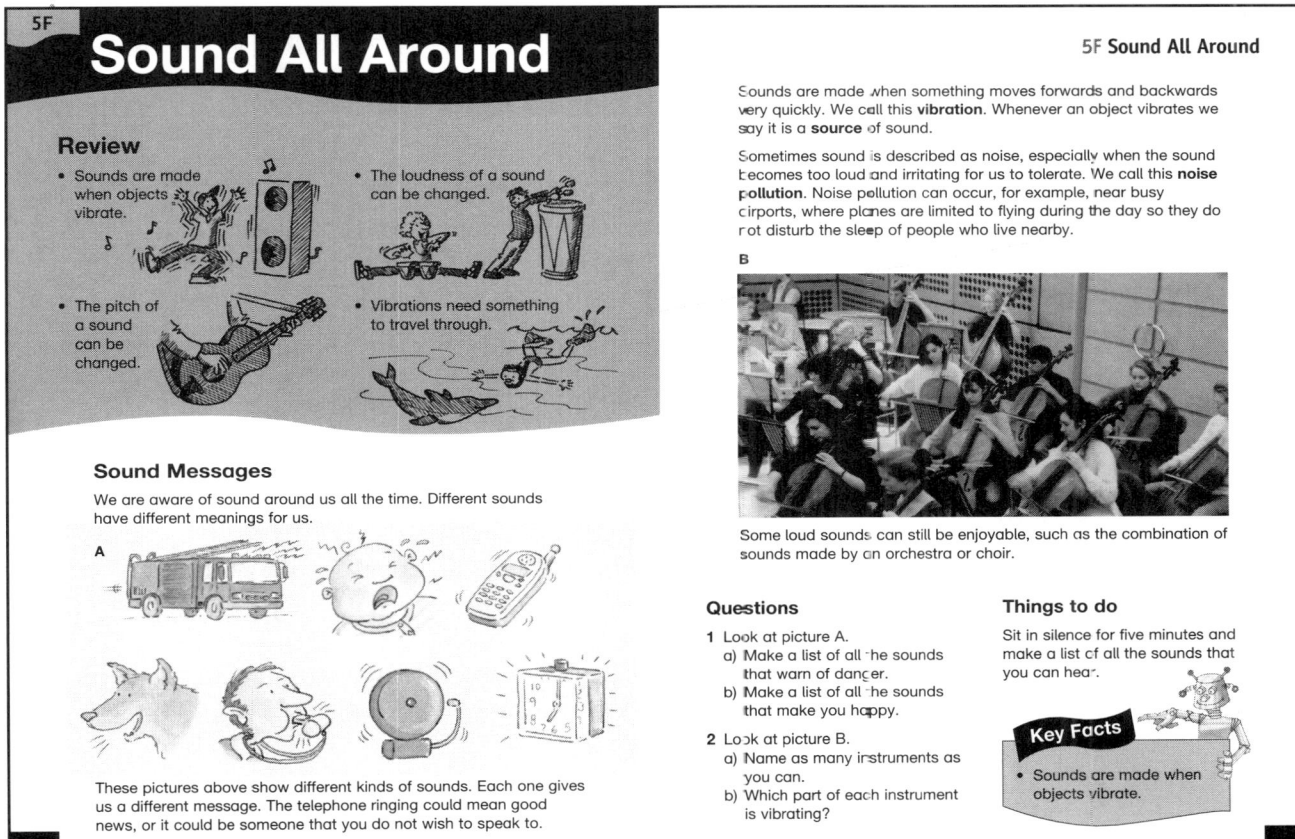

Questions

Questions at the bottom of the page relate directly to the information on the single or double page. Generally the later questions are harder than the earlier ones. They can be used as a basis for whole-class discussion, or for individual or small-group work.

Remember/Key Facts box

This box includes the key facts and ideas that the pupils should be able to recall.

Review

In Years 5 and 6 a set of illustrated facts are given at the beginning of each unit. This information should help to prompt pupils' pre-requisite knowledge needed for the unit.

What Is the Approach to Scientific Enquiry (Sc1) in Science Directions?

In the National Curriculum, Scientific Enquiry is presented as two themes:

• Ideas and Evidence in Science;

• Investigative Skills.

Both themes emphasise the importance of pupils finding evidence to test their ideas. The first theme also highlights the importance of pupils being encouraged to think creatively when putting forward explanations and establishing links between causes and effects. The investigative skills are grouped under the following strands:

• planning;

• obtaining and presenting evidence;

• considering evidence and evaluating.

In each unit of work, there will be many opportunities for pupils to practise and develop their investigative skills. Many activities are investigational in nature. In some, the focus will be on the 'planning' strand, whereas in others the focus will be on the 'obtaining and presenting evidence' strand or the 'considering evidence and evaluating' strand. In every unit, there is at least one activity that encourages a whole investigation approach, i.e. one in which all three strands are covered. In almost all of the units, the whole investigation is presented as the Key Activity.

The Key Activity comes at the end of the unit when all the key ideas and concepts of the unit have been covered. Pupils are then able to apply their knowledge and understanding in an investigational context. A writing frame is often included as one of the photocopiable masters in order to help the pupils to structure their work.

The following table identifies the key features of Sc1 for each National Curriculum level.

Key Features

Level	Planning	Obtaining and Presenting	Considering and Evaluating
1		• make simple descriptions by talking or drawing.	• talk about the work.
2	• make suggestions with help; • find information from simple texts.	• make simple descriptions; • make comparisons; • use simple equipment; • use simple tables.	• compare findings with expectations.
3	• put forward own ideas without help.	• measure quantities; • perform a fair test with help.	• identify simple patterns; • provide simple conclusions; • provide explanations; • suggest improvements.
4	• decide on an approach, e.g. fair tests; • make simple predictions; • select information from provided sources.	• make a series of observations and measurements; • select suitable equipment; • draw tables, bar charts and simple line graphs.	• interpret patterns; • link conclusions to knowledge and understanding; • suggest improvements with reasons.
5	• identify key factors; • make predictions based on scientific knowledge and understanding; • select from a range of sources of information.	• repeat observations and measurements to improve reliability; • use line graphs independently.	• draw conclusions consistent with the evidence, and relate to scientific knowledge and understanding.

Each of the key features can be seen as being indicative of an overall level of attainment. In an investigation, a pupil does not need to demonstrate all the key features associated with a particular level before that level can be awarded. For example, a pupil who plans a fair test could be judged to be at Level 4 in the planning strand even though she may not have made a prediction. In addition, although the investigation may have provided opportunities to show attainment in all three strands, for assessment purposes it is perfectly reasonable to focus on just one of the strands, e.g. planning. Further details are given in the section How Should I Assess the Pupils' Work? on page 35.

The titles of the whole investigations included in Years 1–6 of Science Directions are listed below:

Unit	Context	Whole Investigation Title
1A	Sc2	Are the Oldest Children the Tallest?
1B	Sc2	Investigating Plant Growth
1C	Sc3	Which is the Best Material to Use for an Umbrella?
1D	Sc4	What Lets Light Through?
1E	Sc4	Which Car Will Travel the Furthest?
1F	Sc4	Moving Messages
2A	Sc2	How Clean Are Your Hands?
2B	Sc2	Exploring Mini-beasts
2C	Sc2	Measuring Hand Spans and Feet
2D	Sc3	Which is the Most Stretchy Rubber Band?
2E	Sc4	Bulldog Buggies
2F	Sc4	(Make a Picture of a Clown)*
3A	Sc2	How Clean Are Your Teeth?
3B	Sc2	Greenhouse Investigation
3C	Sc3	Which is the Strongest Paper to Use for Paper Bags?
3D	Sc3	Comparing the Permeability of Different Types of Soil
3E	Sc4	Investigating Catapults
3F	Sc4	Transparency Investigation
4A	Sc2	Do People With the Longest Legs Jump the Furthest or the Highest?
4B	Sc2	Habitat Help
4C	Sc3	Which is the Best Insulator?
4D	Sc3	Investigating Dissolving
4E	Sc4	Which Shoes Give the Best Grip?
4F	Sc4	What Affects the Brightness of a Bulb?
5A	Sc2	Energy and Exercise
5B	Sc2	Investigating the Germination and Growth of Seedlings
5C	Sc3	Investigating Insulators
5D	Sc3	How Air Flow Affects Evaporation
5E	Sc4	Investigating Balloon Rockets
5F	Sc4	Soundproofing
6A	Sc2	What do Mini-beasts Prefer?
6B	Sc2	Yeast
6C	Sc3	How Temperature Affects How Quickly Sugar Dissolves
6D	Sc3	Factors That Affect the Burning of a Candle
6E	Sc4	Investigating Spinners
6F	Sc4	Investigating the Size of Shadows
6G	Sc4	How Does the Length of Wire in a Circuit Affect the Brightness of a Bulb?

* The content of the unit does not lend itself to a whole investigation.

How Are Key Concepts Developed through Science Directions?

Key concepts are developed progressively through the Science Directions units. A particular concept may be developed in a number of different units in the same year or it may be developed from year to year. The theme charts indicate where the concepts are first introduced and the opportunities that subsequently arise for consolidation and extension.

 Please see photocopiable theme charts within the Support Materials on pages 75–88.

Theme: Changing Materials (Sc3)

Unit	Activity	Heating Materials	Mixing Materials	Temperature	Reversible Changes	Non-reversible Changes
EY Seasonal Activities	Ice Cold Animals	•				
EY Cooking and Food	Banana Bread	•	•			
	Fruity Drinks		•			
	A Big Breakfast		•			
	One Potato, Two Potato	•				
EY Art Activities	Mixing and Painting		•			
	Drippy Pictures		•			
2D Grouping and Changing Materials	3 Heating Materials (1)	•				
	4 Heating Materials (2)	•				
	5 Melting Ice	•				
3C Characteristics of Materials	5 Which Substances Melt?	•			•	
4C Keeping Warm	1 Temperature			•	•	
	2 Measuring Temperature Around the School			•		
4D Solids and Liquids	2 Changing Solids to Liquids	•			•	
	3 Adding Solids to Water: Dissolving		•		•	
	6 Investigating Dissolving		•		•	
5C Gases All Around	3 Evaporation	•			•	
5D Changing State	1 States of Matter and Processes				•	
	2 Changing Ice	•			•	
	3 The Water Cycle	•			•	
6C More About Dissolving	5 Factors Affecting Dissolving		•		•	
	6 How Temperature Affects How Quickly Sugar Dissolves		•		•	
6D Reversible and Irreversible Changes	1 Classifying Changes				•	•
	2 Burning as an Irreversible Change					•
	3 What Factors Affect the Burning of a Candle?					•

How Can Science Directions Help me in my Role as Subject Leader?

The National Standards for Subject Leaders were published by the Teacher Training Agency in 1998. These standards specify the four key areas of subject leadership:

A. Strategic direction and development of the subject;
B. Teaching and learning;
C. Leading and managing staff;
D. Efficient and effective deployment of staff and resources.

Within these key areas there are a number of crucial roles for the subject leader.

Crucial Roles of a Subject Leader	Co-ordinator's Handbook
Analyse and interpret relevant national, local and school data, plus research and inspection evidence, to inform policies, practices, expectations, targets and teaching methods. (Av)	How Should I Monitor and Evaluate the Quality of Pupils' Work? (page 38)
Monitor the progress made in achieving subject plans and targets, evaluate the effects on teaching and learning, and use this analysis to guide further improvement. (Avii)	How Should I Monitor and Evaluate the Quality of Pupils' Work? (page 38)
Ensure curriculum coverage, continuity and progression in the subject for all pupils, including those of high ability and those with special educational or linguistic needs. (Bi)	How Should I Approach Differentiation? (page 27)
Ensure that teachers are clear about the teaching objectives in lessons, understand the sequence of teaching and learning in the subject, and communicate such information to pupils. (Bii)	How Should I Plan? (page 23)
Ensure effective development of pupils' literacy, numeracy and information technology skills through the subject. (Biv)	How Can I Develop Literacy, Numeracy and ICT Skills? (page 29)
Establish and implement clear policies and practices for assessing, recording and reporting on pupil achievement, and for using this information to recognise achievement and to assist pupils in setting targets for further improvements. (Bv)	How Should I Assess the Pupils' Work? (page 35)
Evaluate the teaching of the subject in the school, use this analysis to identify effective practice and areas for improvement, and take action to improve further the quality of teaching. (Bviii)	How Should I Monitor and Evaluate the Quality of Pupils' Work? (page 38)
Lead professional development of subject staff through example and support. (Cvi)	Co-ordinator OHPs and photocopiable masters (see Support Materials pages 45–88) **SM 1–18**
Ensure the effective and efficient management and organisation of learning resources, including information and communications technology. (Diii)	How Should I Manage Resources? (page 33)
Ensure that there is a safe working and learning environment in which risks are properly assessed. (Dvi)	What Are my Responsibilities for Safety? (page 34)

How Should I Plan?

Planning is most easily considered at three levels: long-, medium- and short-term. The characteristics of each level of planning and the support offered by Science Directions are included in the table below.

Level of Planning	Key Features	Link to Science Directions
long-term	• organisation and sequencing of the programme of study for a whole year or key stage into units of study; • allocation of time to each unit of study; • organisation of approach to particular aspects, e.g. scientific enquiry (Sc1), assessment, etc.	All features are included in the Teaching Files and the Co-ordinator's Handbook.
medium-term	• usually organised unit by unit; • provides details of pupils' prior experience; • provides a range of expected learning outcomes for pupils; • provides detailed activities through which the learning outcomes can be achieved; • identifies appropriate assessment opportunities.	Comprehensive medium-term plans are included for each unit in the Teaching File.
short-term	• concerned with the day-to-day organisation of the classroom, including the specific learning outcomes targeted, the grouping of pupils, organisation of resources, etc.	Teachers will need to produce their own short-term plans. See page 26 for an example.

Long-Term Planning

In order for a long-term plan to be coherent, it should satisfy a number of criteria. Does it provide:

• opportunities for pupils to study Sc2, 3, and 4 every year?

• opportunities for the pupils to practise the skills of Sc1 regularly?

• opportunities to revisit key ideas and concepts in order to consolidate and extend learning?

• links to other areas of the school curriculum, e.g. citizenship, literacy, numeracy, ICT?

An example of a typical long-term plan is shown on the following page.

A Long-Term Plan for a Primary School

Year	Autumn	Spring	Summer
1	1A Ourselves 1F Sound and Hearing	1D Light and Dark 1C Sorting and Using Materials	1B Growing Plants 1E Pushes and Pulls
2	2B Plants and Animals in the Local Environment 2F Using Electricity	2D Grouping and Changing Materials 2E Forces and Movement	2A Health and Growth 2C Variation
3	3A Teeth and Eating 3F Light and Shadows	3E Magnets and Springs 3C Characteristics of Materials	3B Helping Plants Grow Well 3D Rocks and Soils
4	4E Friction 4F Circuits and Conductors	4C Keeping Warm 4D Solids and Liquids	4A Moving and Growing 4B Habitats
5	5C Gases All Around 6G Changing Circuits 5E Earth, Sun and Moon	5D Changing State 5A Keeping Healthy	5F Sound All Around 5B Life Cycles 6B Micro-organisms
6	6C More About Dissolving 6D Reversible and Irreversible Changes 6F How We See Things	6A Interdependence and Adaptation 6E Forces in Action Growth and Reproduction (School devised unit to link with PSD)	Revision

The example illustrates a long-term plan for a primary school that has single-year classes. In this case, the Science Directions units have been allocated to the terms of the year, taking seasonal factors and traditional events that take place within the school into account. For example, Unit 4B, Habitats, has been scheduled for the summer term, reflecting a school tradition of visiting a sea shore habitat for a joint science/geography fieldwork day. The school has also organised the units to allow time to revise for the Key Stage 2 SATs. In order to do this, the shorter units of work in Year 6 (6B, 6D, 6F and 6G) have been matched with other units of work throughout Years 5 and 6. This school completes a bridging project with the local high school after the tests in Year 6. An alternative to this is to teach Unit 5/6H, Enquiry in Environmental and Technological Contexts, as supplied by QCA.

Science Directions has been written to be flexible enough for units to be taught in any order in each of the two-year cycles of Years 1/2, 3/4 and 5/6. So, for example, for a mixed Year 1/2 class, one year, the Year 1 pupils would start with the Year 1 units, while the following year, the Year 1 pupils would start with the Year 2 units. If a school with mixed age classes wishes to combine units across the year pairs shown above, this is possible but care should be taken to change the learning outcomes according to the year group. For example, if Unit 3A, Teeth and Eating, is taught to a mixed Year 2/3 class, the learning outcomes and teaching activities should be adapted to take into account those pupils who are attaining within Level 1. (The learning outcomes and activities for this unit are designed to be aimed between Levels 2 and 4.)

Medium-Term Planning

Science Directions provides very comprehensive medium-term plans for each unit of work. The units include learning objectives that are derived from the National Curriculum programmes of study, and associated activities, which are described in great detail. Each unit of work also provides learning outcomes that are linked to the National Curriculum level descriptions. In essence, the Teaching Files are the medium-term plans!

Throughout the year, individual teachers may find alternative ways of teaching certain activities. Teachers should be encouraged to annotate the activity descriptions in the Teaching File when appropriate. However, they should be wary of incorporating alternative activities before checking with the subject leader or co-ordinator that these activities do not appear in other units and years. At the end of the year, each unit should be reviewed and any changes incorporated for future years.

Short-Term Planning

This is the responsibility of the individual class teacher. This level of planning takes into account the needs of groups and individual pupils within the class. Essentially any short-term plan should contain:

- short-term learning objectives derived from the medium-term plan;
- key teaching points;
- the organisation of groups and individual pupils within the class;
- the use being made of parent and teaching assistant support (if applicable);
- assessment opportunities;
- the use of resources;
- ways of reviewing what the pupils have learnt during the activity.

Many schools have a common format for short-term planning. An example is given here and on page 74 of what a short-term plan may look like.

Summerside Primary School: Short-term Plan for Science

Date   01.04.01   **Time**   Tuesday 1.30pm. 1.5 hrs

Objectives	Activities
From Science Directions Teaching File 2, page 41, Forces and Movement	Together, all pupils will discuss water-mills and windmills and will be questioned about how they work. Establish that it is the force of the wind or water that makes them move.
• *Pupils will be able to describe how wind and water can produce a force.*	Show them the resources and challenge them to make a waterwheel or a windmill.
	Pupils to work in pairs – not George and Joe together.
Resources	Green and red table to make windmills.
As page 41, Pupil Book pages 34 and 35	Mrs Brown, the TA, will work with blue table on water wheels.
	Yellow table also to make water wheels.
	Ask the pupils how they could test the effectiveness of their wheels. Each group to demonstrate how they work and talk about the forces that they are using.
	Plenary
	Use the Pupil Book to answer questions about the force of water.

This plan is for a Year 2 class. If it had been for older children, the plan may also have contained advice on the assessment of individual pupils, as well as details of extension activities and homework opportunities.

How Should I Approach Differentiation?

In teaching and learning situations, the word 'differentiation' refers to the presentation of tasks at different conceptual or reading levels, or in different contexts, in order to give all pupils full access to the curriculum. When planning for differentiation, there are some key principles that should be considered:

- all learners are different and learn in different ways;
- knowing individual pupils well is the key to good differentiation;
- the fact that something has been taught does not mean that it has been learnt;
- every class is a mixed ability group.

Learners can be different in a number of ways. They can have different:

- abilities;
- skill levels;
- prior experiences;
- expectations;
- interests.

Catering for all these differences in a class of 30 pupils seems a rather daunting task! There is clearly a limit to how much consideration should be given to these differences when teaching a class. Science Directions has adopted an approach that is manageable and helps a teacher to:

Establish clear learning outcomes, which cover the range of attainment within the class

For each unit of work, learning outcomes have been identified at three different levels of attainment. Essentially these represent the expected attainment, below average attainment and above average attainment for the particular year group being taught.

Identify the prior experiences of the pupils and their current levels of knowledge and understanding

Science Directions is a comprehensive scheme for 3–11-year-olds and, as such, prior experiences can be quickly checked (see the theme charts on pages 75–87). In addition, the first teaching activity in each unit has been specifically designed as an orientation activity, i.e. one that will provide opportunities for the teacher to find out the extent of prior knowledge and understanding. This is done in a wide range of ways including the use of demonstrations, card-sorting activities, concept mapping, etc. In all cases, the pupils are encouraged to present and talk about their ideas.

Use a variety of strategies for differentiation

Questioning

Within the teaching activities, emphasis is placed on the types of questions that can be used and these are clearly highlighted. Questioning is a key factor in differentiation. One minute it can be used to support and encourage those pupils who lack confidence and understanding; the next, it can be used to extend and challenge those pupils who have a good understanding. Current research on the use of questioning to support learning is well worth reading.* One interesting line of research suggests that asking a pupil a series of linked questions is far more effective in developing understanding than using single questions directed to different pupils.

By Task

Pupils can be given different tasks that match their level of attainment or preferred learning styles. In some cases, all pupils can be given the same basic task but receive different amounts of support, for example, through the use of worksheets and writing frames. Many of the photocopiable masters included in the Teaching Files can be used in this way. Writing frames are included in each unit to support pupils in their investigative work. For some pupils, these will quickly become unnecessary; for others, they will remain a crucial support.

Many of the teaching activities finish with a Pupil Consolidation section. This provides suggestions of other tasks and activities to give the pupils to consolidate their learning. In many cases, these activities are intended to broaden and extend understanding. As such, they are more likely to be used with selected groups of pupils than with the whole class.

By Outcome

In this case, the task needs to be open-ended, so allowing for different levels of response. One of the drawbacks of this approach is that some pupils have low aspirations and consequently their expectations are not high enough. This problem can be overcome by ensuring that pupils are aware of the learning outcomes they are expected to achieve. The whole investigations, included in each Science Directions unit as the Key Activity, facilitate this particular approach to differentiation.

By Intervention

Not surprisingly, the teacher's involvement with the pupils is crucial in ensuring effective differentiation. More and more, teaching assistants are also fulfilling this role. Intervening, whether in group or individual work, enables a constant reappraisal of the learning process, and modifications can be made as appropriate.

*Black, P and William, D, (1998) *Inside the black box: Raising standards through classroom assessment*, School of Education, King's College.

Assessment Reform Group, (1999) *Assessment for Learning: Beyond the black box*, University of Cambridge School of Education.

How Can I Develop Literacy, Numeracy and ICT Skills?

Literacy

Science Directions provides many opportunities for pupils to express themselves through speaking and writing. The format of the teaching activities, with its emphasis on questioning, encourages the pupils to engage in discussion and to share their ideas both in small groups and with the whole class. In terms of the development of writing skills, pupils have opportunities to:

- write in a variety of genres including reports, instructions, lists, letters and play scripts, making use of scientific vocabulary;

- use charts;

- label diagrams;

- provide descriptions, explanations and evaluations;

- draft, edit and refine.

Part of the skill of working scientifically is to be able to write for a particular audience, and express opinions and findings with clarity. The science activities the pupils engage in provide a real context and purpose for their writing. However, it is important that the pupils are not always asked to write about their work. In some instances, talking about what they have discovered will be sufficient. A balance has to be found; too often, science is associated with repetitive, extended pieces of writing.

Science Directions suggests a variety of approaches to writing and recording in the teaching activities within the Teaching Files. In addition, through the use of the photocopiable masters, pupils will experience a full range of writing styles and purposes. As the course develops, the demands increase progressively. For example:

- In Key Stage 1, the pupils are given the task of producing a list as a means of recording the different ways a ball moves (2E PM1) or that of adding labels to a prepared diagram (1B PM1).

- In Key Stage 2, pupils are encouraged to become more independent in their work. The photocopiable masters provide greater opportunities for the pupils to record work in their own way. There is also a greater emphasis on the use of scientific vocabulary. In Years 5 and 6, pupils are encouraged to use a glossary, provided in the Pupil's Books, to support the accuracy of their writing.

- Pupils in Key Stage 2 are expected to be able to argue for and against specific proposals, drawing on their scientific knowledge and understanding. This approach can be found, for example, in the habitats work in Year 4. Drama and role-play have also been included to encourage pupils to understand the work of famous scientists. This approach can be seen in Unit 6B, Micro-organisms, where the pupils re-enact the story of Edward Jenner and discuss the ethics of experimentation on living things.

- In each unit, a writing frame is included as one of the photocopiable masters. These are intended to provide support for pupils' writing and so develop confidence. In order for the pupils to get the most benefit from using the frame, the teacher should model its use and support pupils as they write on their own copies. An enlarged frame positioned centrally in the classroom can be used for this purpose.

Numeracy

Scientists use mathematics as a tool to enable them to measure and present their findings and data. In Science Directions, numerical skills are developed progressively:

- Early work at Key Stage 1 provides pupils with a context for making comparisons. Pupils at this stage are also encouraged to make drawings and maps which, though not necessarily to scale, provide the early experiences of scale drawings.

- At this stage, the pupils are also encouraged to gather data in early survey work, whether on the ways in which animals move, or on favourite food types.

- Pupils are encouraged to use standard measures and units from an early age, for example, when measuring length. Temperature is used as a comparative measure in Key Stage 1, but is developed quantitatively by using a thermometer in Key Stage 2. The newton as a measurement of force is introduced in Year 4 and further extended in Year 6.

- Towards the end of Key Stage 2, pupils are encouraged to take repeated readings and then calculate the median or average to ensure greater accuracy.

- Graphical work is introduced in Key Stage 1 through the use of simple charts and tables. Bar charts and line graphs are used to present findings from the beginning of Key Stage 2. The Sc1 investigative work developed through the Key Activity in each unit provides extensive opportunities for developing graphical work as part of the 'obtaining and presenting evidence' strand. Pupils should be encouraged to 'tell the story of the line' in order to improve their understanding of this form of analysing data.

- Work on Scientific Enquiry in the Year 6 Pupil Book ensures that pupils can practice interpreting bar charts and line graphs prior to taking their exams at the end of Key Stage 2.

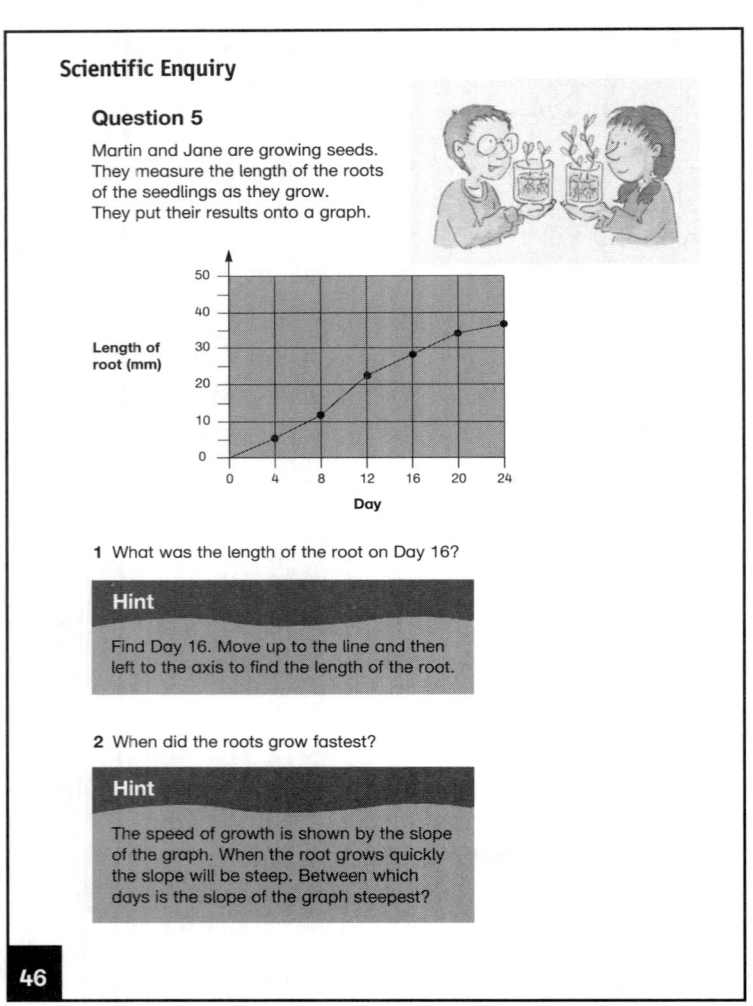

Scientific Enquiry

Question 5

Martin and Jane are growing seeds. They measure the length of the roots of the seedlings as they grow. They put their results onto a graph.

1 What was the length of the root on Day 16?

Hint

Find Day 16. Move up to the line and then left to the axis to find the length of the root.

2 When did the roots grow fastest?

Hint

The speed of growth is shown by the slope of the graph. When the root grows quickly the slope will be steep. Between which days is the slope of the graph steepest?

46

Information and Communications Technology (ICT)

"Pupils use ICT tools to find, explore, analyse, exchange and present information responsibly, creatively and with discrimination. They learn how to employ ICT to enable rapid access to ideas and experiences from a wide range of people, communities and cultures."

The National Curriculum, 1999.

During Key Stage 1, pupils should start to use ICT to develop their ideas and record their work. In Key Stage 2, pupils should develop their research skills and decide what information is appropriate for their work. They should begin to question the quality of the information they find.

In the National Curriculum for ICT, the knowledge, skills and understanding are presented under four themes:

1 Finding Things Out	• searching the internet or a CD-ROM; • using printed material; • using databases.	
2 Developing Ideas and Making Things Happen	• desktop publishing; • multimedia presentations; • using sensors; • simulations.	
3 Exchanging and Sharing Information	• displays; • posters.	
4 Reviewing, Modifying and Evaluating Work as it Progresses		

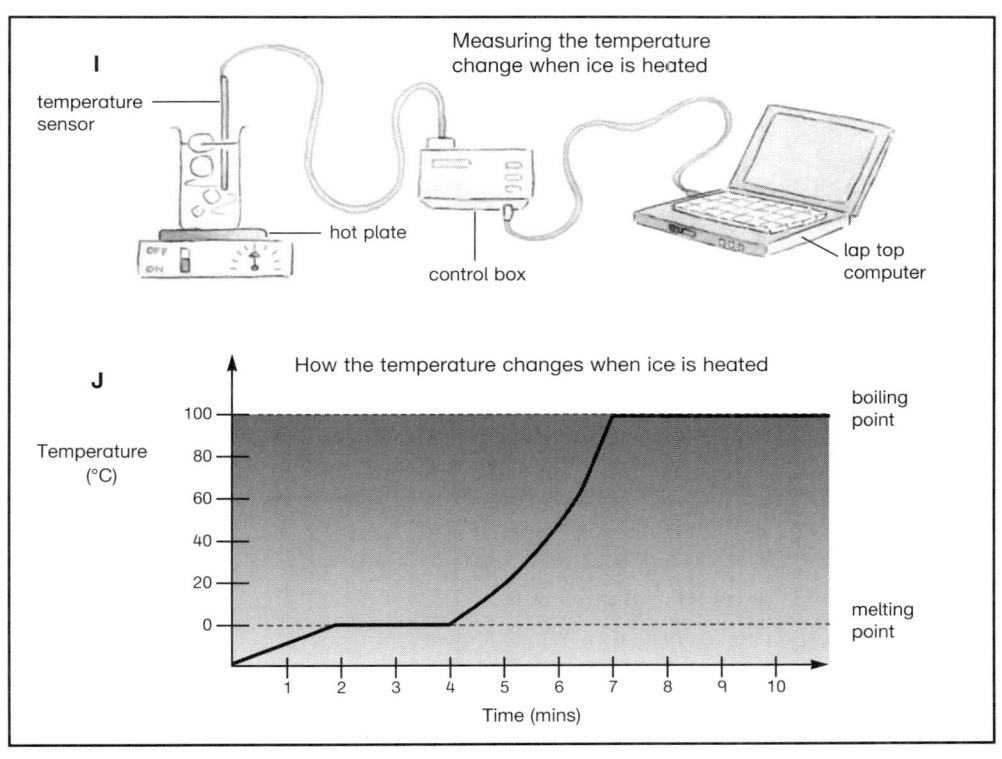

I temperature sensor, hot plate, control box, lap top computer

Measuring the temperature change when ice is heated

J How the temperature changes when ice is heated

There are numerous opportunities within Science Directions for pupils to experience themes 3 and 4. Specific opportunities for developing themes 1 and 2 are identified in the table below.

Unit	Activity	Theme
1D	3 The Black Box	1
1F	4 Instrument Data Search	1
2A	2 Favourite Food Survey	1
2B	4 Animal Life Cycles	1
2D	2 Natural Materials	1
3A	3 Pet-food Survey	1
3B	1 Virtual Greengrocers	1
3B	4 Greenhouse Investigation	1
3D	1 Rocks as Natural Materials	1
3D	3 Comparing the Hardness and Permeability of Rocks	1
3D	4 Research into Different Types of Rock	1
3E	1 Forces	1
3E	3 Which is the Strongest Magnet?	1
3F	4 Sun Movement	1
3F	6 Transparency Investigation	2
4A	1 Bone Location	1
4A	3 Skeletons of Other Animals	1
4A	4 Muscles	1
4B	1 Picture Sort	1
4B	3 Invertebrate Survey	1
4C	2 Measuring Temperature Around the School	2
4C	3 Keeping Things Hot	1
4C	4 Thermal Insulators	1
4E	4 Streamlining	1
5A	1 What is Health?	1
5A	3 Drugs and Smoking	1
5B	2 Seed Dispersal	1
5C	1 Solids, Liquids and Gases	1
5C	4 Common Gases	1
5D	2 Changing Ice	2
5D	3 The Water Cycle	1
5D	5 Purifying Water	1
5E	1 Stars and Planets	1
5E	2 The Universe	1
5E	5 The Moon	1
5F	6 Soundproofing	2
6A	1 The Needs of Plants Revisited	2
6A	4 Different Habitats	1
6B	1 What Makes us Ill?	1
6E	2 Gravity	1
6F	1 Shadows	1

How Should I Manage Resources?

Due to the specialist nature of some of the resources used in science, and the fact that they are used infrequently, it makes sense to store the majority of the resources centrally. Depending on the size of the school, this central storage could service all classes or, alternatively, there could be a central resource for each key stage. In addition, there are a number of regularly used resources that can be stored in each classroom. It is also useful to have single sets of equipment that can be used for reference and demonstration by the teacher. A list of such items is given below:

Classroom Science Resource List

General Items

writing paper

squared paper/graph paper

sugar paper

paper towels

card

coloured pens

string

scissors

rulers

Post-it notes

glue

Sellotape

Blu-tack

rubber bands

Science Items

hand lenses

measuring tapes

torch

magnet

tweezers

soft paint brush

mini-viewer for mini-beasts

candle/night light and matches

night light holder

(cells, wires, crocodile clips for a simple circuit)

To facilitate the efficient ordering, organisation and storage of resources, the resource requirements for Science Directions for each year are listed in the Support Materials on pages 45 to 59.

SM
1-7

What Are my Responsibilities for Safety?

Before undertaking any activity, a teacher must make a risk assessment. This means that consideration should be given to:

- the potential hazards of the materials to be used;

- the group of pupils that will be using the materials.

A consequence of this is that, having assessed the risk, a teacher may undertake an activity with one group of pupils and not with another, or decide that one group will need close supervision when undertaking the activity, whereas another will not. Within Science Directions, specific risks associated with materials, or their suggested use, are clearly highlighted. However, it is the teacher's responsibility to assess the overall risk in the context of the pupils who will be undertaking the activity.

 **Safety**
Great care should be taken when smelling volatile liquids. Many of them are toxic.
It is recommended that you use air fresheners (or perfume atomisers) only.

The National Curriculum programme of study states that pupils should be taught to:

"use simple equipment and materials appropriately and take action to control risks".

It is good practice to ask the pupils to consider the risks involved when undertaking a practical activity and then to discuss the precautions they should take to minimise the risk.

The Association for Science Education publication *Be Safe* (ISBN 0 86357 081X) provides a comprehensive list of risk assessments and, as such, is a useful source of reference. In addition, your own LEA may have adopted certain local restrictions on the use of particular materials. These are usually published in Health and Safety documentation. If in doubt, ask your LEA Health and Safety Officer for details.

Some frequently asked safety questions follow:

Question	Answer (unless other local restrictions apply)
• Can I use glassware in my classroom?	Yes, but the potential hazards should be discussed with the pupils.
• What kind of thermometer can I use?	Most kinds. LCD strips are useful for body temperature, and alcohol 'stirring' thermometers are good for heating and cooling activities. In addition, there are a range of digital thermometers available. **Do not** use mercury thermometers unless there is a mercury spill kit available.
• Are candles banned?	No, but always use a sand tray to stand them in. Night light candles are more stable and will be suitable for most uses.

How Should I Assess the Pupils' Work?

Science Directions has been designed on the premise that regular assessment of pupil attainment is desirable, and associated feedback to pupils on their progress is important. There is a renewed national focus on the use of classroom assessment strategies to improve teaching and learning. Research evidence suggests that assessment *for* learning (as opposed to assessment *of* learning) is very important in raising standards. Teachers need to be clear how day-to-day activities and informal observations can be used to identify the strengths and needs of the pupils.

The characteristics of assessment that promote learning can be summarised as follows:

- it involves sharing learning goals with pupils;
- it supports pupils in recognising the standards they are aiming for;
- it involves pupils in self-assessment;
- it provides feedback to pupils, which identifies the next steps to take.

In this context, two key aspects of effective teaching include:

- the use of questions to find out what pupils understand;
- the use of feedback and marking to help to advance learning.

Science Directions has been developed in such a way as to support these key aspects of effective teaching. Specific questions have been highlighted in the Teaching Files, and the organisation of the work into individual activities – supported by photocopiable masters – facilitates the making of regular judgements of attainment and associated feedback to pupils.

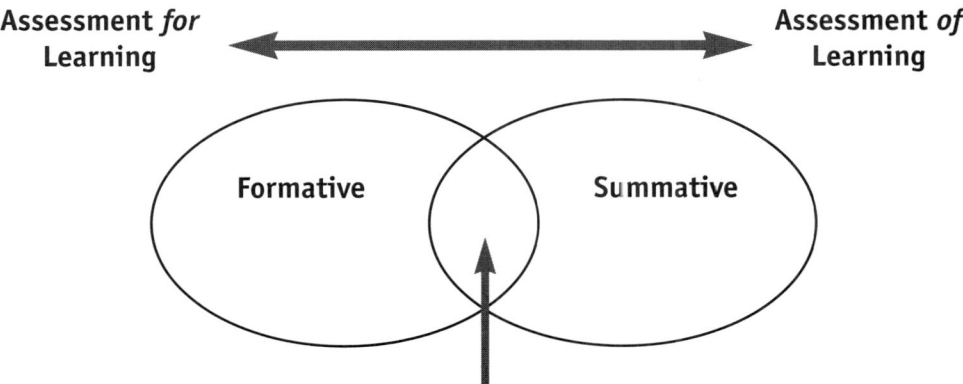

Schools can exploit the overlap to use ongoing classroom assessments to make more regular judgements that will help in reviewing progress.

Level Descriptions

National Curriculum levels are defined by a series of level descriptors. A pupil judged to be attaining Level 3 in Physical Processes (Sc4) does not need to have satisfied all the requirements of that level. It does mean, however, that the pupil's attainment is more closely matched by the level descriptors in Level 3 than those in Level 2 or in Level 4. In other words, the levels are intended to be used in a 'best fit' approach rather than one which signifies 'mastery'. As a direct result of this, the levels can be used to support ongoing or formative assessment, as well as summative or terminal assessment.

Assessment Requirements

The statutory requirements for assessment, recording and reporting include the following aspects:

- to provide an annual report to parents on individual progress in relation to the National Curriculum;

- to update the pupil's educational record annually;

- to fulfil the requirements of the end-of-key-stage assessments.

In addition to these requirements, teachers will want to provide continuous feedback to pupils on their progress, and set targets for improvement. This can be done orally and through the marking of the pupils' work. However, there are some important questions that need to be considered:

- What form should the marking take?

- How should the marking relate to the learning outcomes specified in the Teaching File?

- To what extent should the assessment of work relate to National Curriculum levels?

Using the statutory requirements as a starting point, it would seem logical to adopt an end-of-year summative recording system that uses National Curriculum levels. This is a statutory requirement at the end of the key stage and it therefore makes sense to adopt this approach at the end of every year.

The end-of-year judgements will be determined by considering the standards achieved by each pupil during the year. The judgements can be made from a general consideration of the pupils' work over the year. However, this is likely to be a much more straightforward process if some interim judgements have been made throughout the year. These interim judgements do not need to be large in number but should relate to significant achievements in particular units of work and arise from what can be called *significant activities*.

Significant Activities

A significant activity is one that requires pupils to apply their skills, knowledge and understanding in a context that is, to some extent, unfamiliar. Within Science Directions, significant activities have been identified for each unit. The Key Activity usually acts as a significant activity for Sc1, and various activities within the Pupil Books and photocopiable masters fulfil the same role for Sc2, 3 and 4. Typical or expected outcomes from these significant activities are given as 'Assessment Pointers' on the Assessment pages in the Teaching Files (see page 16). To ensure that the on-going assessment remains manageable the number of significant activities chosen per unit needs to be limited, e.g. one for Sc1 and one or two for the knowledge-based attainment target (Sc2, 3 or 4). Using these significant activities, and associated Assessment Pointers, it is possible to take a 'snapshot' of pupil achievement on a unit-by-unit basis, and record these in terms of National Curriculum levels.

When using the Key Activity to assess pupils' progress in Sc1, it is not always necessary to assess performance in all three strands ('planning', 'obtaining and presenting evidence', 'considering evidence and evaluating') and then work out an overall level. An alternative, and equally acceptable approach, is to assess performance in just one strand. If this approach is adopted, it is important that, taking all the units as a whole, equal emphasis is given to all the strands.

Incorporating this idea of significant activities into the teaching approach ensures that in each unit of work pupils can be given detailed feedback on their progress against the expected learning outcomes. The other marking undertaken in the unit may be different and is likely to focus on:

● the completeness of the work;

● presentation;

● general accuracy.

A Class Science Recording Sheet is included to illustrate how the approach described in this section can be used to generate a profile of attainment for each pupil (see page 73).

Class Science Recording Sheet

| Class | | | | | Teacher | | | | | | | | | | | | | | | | | |

Name	Previous Year					Unit A		Unit B		Unit C		Unit D		Unit E		Unit F		Unit G		End of Year				
	Sc1	Sc2	Sc3	Sc4	Sc all	Sc1 poc	Sc 234	Sc1 poc	Sc 234	Sc1 poc	Sc 234	Sc1 poc	Sc 234	Sc1 poc	Sc 234	Sc1 poc	Sc 234	Sc1 poc	Sc 234	Sc1	Sc2	Sc3	Sc4	Sc all

Note for Sc1: planning (p); obtaining and presenting evidence (o); considering evidence and evaluating (c).

Science Directions Co-ordinator's Handbook Photocopiable Master · HarperCollinsPublishers Ltd 2001

73

SM 14

How Should I Monitor and Evaluate the Quality of Work in Science?

Monitoring requires that relevant information is collected about the quality of work being undertaken in science. Evaluation is concerned with making judgements based on the evidence collected. Monitoring and evaluating work in science is not just about observing colleagues teaching their lessons. This is an important part of the overall quality assurance process but there are a number of other aspects to consider. The monitoring and evaluating process can be considered to involve three distinct factors:

- Input Factors: these include a consideration of teachers' plans.
- Process Factors: these include lesson observation.
- Output Factors: these include a consideration of pupils' own views, their work and their test results.

Input Factors

There is obviously a clear link between the quality of pupil outcomes and the quality of teacher planning. Planning needs to be considered at three levels: long-term, medium-term and short-term. The required elements of each of these levels of planning are included in the section How Should I Plan? on page 23.

As subject leader or co-ordinator, it is important to have an overview of the whole course. Teachers will be tempted to incorporate additional or replacement activities into the units of work. While this is generally to be encouraged, it is important that activities which may be included in other units are not incorporated without assessing the overall implications. As the medium-term plans are included in the Teaching Files, there is little point monitoring these. However, checking on changes and adaptations is worthwhile.

Process Factors

Lesson observation is an important means of monitoring and evaluating the quality of the science work being undertaken in the school. Some of the observation will be undertaken by the science co-ordinator or subject leader; other observation may be undertaken by members of the school senior management team. Before observing a lesson, it is important that the teacher being observed:

- is aware when the observation is due to take place;
- knows what the focus of the observation is;
- understands the mechanism for obtaining feedback.

It is also useful to have an agreed list of the features of effective teaching and learning. Possible lists are given on the following page:

Characteristics of Effective Teaching

Teachers display:

- secure knowledge and understanding of the subject (planning, exposition, questioning and marking);

- high expectation and challenge (realistic and matched to ability; learning activities; emphasis on involvement, accuracy, critical thinking, presentation; responsibility);

- good planning (clear learning objectives, differentiation, assessment, resources);

- appropriate methods and organisation (matched to learning objectives and pupil needs);

- good classroom management (high expectations of behaviour, motivation);

- good use of time (appropriate pace and structure);

- constructive assessment (feedback, praise, encouragement, targets set);

- appropriate use of homework to reinforce or extend.

Characteristics of Effective Learning and Response in Lessons

Pupils:

- sustain concentration;

- maintain active involvement (well motivated, show perseverance, answer questions);

- select and use resources critically;

- apply ideas in new contexts;

- show capacity for independent work (pose questions, show initiative);

- behave well (dependable, handle materials and equipment carefully);

- collaborate in groups (respect the views of others);

- take responsibility.

Output Factors

Pupils' Views

The pupils' own views about their progress and the work they are doing are often illuminating! These can be collected informally, although on some occasions they could be collected more formally, for example, using a questionnaire. Typical questions that can be asked are shown below:

Pupil Evaluation

In this unit:

- What activity did you enjoy the most?

- What activity did you enjoy the least?

- What do you think you have learnt?

- What parts did you find hard to understand?

- Are there things you would have liked to have spent more time on?

Work Scrutiny

Undertaking a work scrutiny is also a very valuable way of monitoring and evaluating the work being done in science. Looking at the development of pupils' work over time provides crucial evidence about achievements and how effectively pupils are learning. The key purposes of a work scrutiny can be summarised as:

- How effectively are pupils learning and making progress?

- Are pupils attaining as well as they should be?

- What are pupils doing well and not so well?

- What are the pupils' attitudes to their work?

- What contribution is the teaching making?

- Are there variations between pupils of different attainments and between teachers?

The scrutiny of work can be done in a science meeting, with all teachers being asked to bring three pieces of pupils' work: one from a high-attaining pupil; one from a pupil of average attainment; and one from a lower-attaining pupil. In order to gauge the progression of work within a school, teachers from different year groups could be asked to bring samples of work from units all related to the same theme, e.g. forces. This type of collaborative exercise will raise issues of consistency of approach, which then can be discussed and, where necessary, solutions can be identified.

Specifically the scrutiny will provide evidence of:

- pupil attainment;

- effective learning;

- effective teaching.

Work Scrutiny	
Characteristics of Effective Learning	**Characteristics of Effective Teaching**

Pupils:
 	
 • understand what they are doing;
 	
 • are clear about what needs to be done;
 	
 • complete the tasks they are set;
 	
 • respond to the comments of the teacher;
 	
 • display a range of learning skills including:
 	
     observing and seeking information;
 	
     looking for patterns and deeper understanding;
 	
     solving problems;
 	
     communicating information and ideas in different ways;
 	
     applying what has been learned in new contexts;
 	
     evaluating work done.
	Teachers:
	
	 • set high expectations and so challenge the pupils;
	
	 • employ methods appropriate to the subject learning objectives;
	
	 • employ methods that are matched to the abilities of the pupils;
	
	 • mark work systematically and constructively, using assessment to inform future learning.

A form for recording the outcomes of a work scrutiny is included in the Support Materials on page 72.

Analysis of Test Scores

Analysis of National Curriculum test results is an important role of the co-ordinator or subject leader. At one level, it will identify the pattern of pupil performance in relation to previous school results, the results of similar schools and the national results. It will also show the relative performance of different gender or ethnic groups. At another level, a detailed analysis of the test papers themselves will identify the topic areas that are causing general difficulty and, therefore, those that require a greater teaching emphasis in the future.

The school results can be compared with those of benchmark schools using the PANDA information, which is sent to schools annually.

How Should I Prepare my Pupils for the SATs?

If pupils are going to do well in the SATs, they will need to have time to revise the content of the programmes of study. In addition, they will need to practise the techniques necessary for answering the questions, particularly those where they are asked to handle and interpret data.

The section on Scientific Enquiry at the end of the Year 6 Pupil's Book provides the pupils with some hints and advice on answering questions about handling and interpreting data. The practice questions have been taken directly from the Year 2000 examination papers. The section has two parts:

- making sense of results;

- making sense of bar charts and graphs.

The advice is provided through Hint Boxes.

Hint: Do this in three stages

1 What happens to the *size* from A to C? Does it increase, decrease or stay the same?

2 What happens to the *time* from A to C? Does it increase, decrease or stay the same?

3 Do size and time both increase, both decrease or does one increase and one decrease from A to C?

When revising with the pupils, it is sensible to make good use of past examination questions. A CD-ROM has been produced by Doublestruck in association with QCA entitled TestBase[*]. Using this CD, it is possible to put together combinations of questions by *topic* and by *level*, with associated mark schemes. In this way, the revision can be focused on particular themes, e.g. forces or electricity, and particular levels of attainment.

It is also helpful if the pupils have some revision sheets that summarise the facts they will need to recall. The following revision aids are included in the Support Materials on pages 60–70 of this Handbook:

- Key Facts for each theme;

- a Glossary of important terms arranged by theme.

[*]Available from TestBase, PO Box 208, Newcastle upon Tyne NE3 1FX (Fax. 0870 9000 403).

Preparing for the SATs: Common Errors

As part of the final preparation for the SAT tests, it is worth spending some time looking at some of the common errors made by pupils.

Aspects of the Programme of Study	Common Errors
General	**Poor knowledge of scientific vocabulary** *Problem:* Pupils don't remember the vocabulary or confuse the meaning of scientific terms. *Solution:* Use the glossaries for Sc2, 3 and 4. Identify the words the pupils have difficulty with and concentrate on these.
Sc1	**Interpreting data and describing relationships between variables** *Problem 1:* Pupils have difficulty in explaining verbally what a bar chart or graph shows. They often misinterpret the scale; for example, if a bar chart has been drawn with a time axis, the quickest time is often interpreted as the longest time, i.e. the biggest bar on the chart. *Problem 2:* Pupils have difficulty in describing a whole pattern. For example, they often say, "the biggest egg takes the longest" rather than "the bigger the egg, the longer it takes to hatch". *Solution:* Use the section on Scientific Enquiry in the Year 6 Pupil Book to practise these skills. **Distinguishing between fair tests and repeated measurements** *Problem:* Pupils often relate the need to repeat readings to the provision of a fair test. *Solution:* Repeated readings are about ensuring the *accuracy* of the measurements. Fair testing is about *controlling variables* that might affect the result of the investigation. The distinction will need to be made by considering investigations the pupils have done; for example, look back at Unit 6E, Investigating Spinners.
Sc2	**Food chains** *Problem:* Pupils often write the food chain the wrong way round: they start with the top consumer and finish with the producer. *Solution:* Recap the work done in Unit 6A, Interdependence and Adaptation. Emphasise that the arrows in the food chain show the movement of the food (energy).

Aspects of the Programme of Study	Common Errors
Sc2	**Life cycles** *Problem:* The sequence of flower production: pollination → germination → seed dispersal, is not well known, with germination, in particular, not being well understood. *Solution:* Revise the work covered in Unit 5B, Life Cycles. **The function of leaves** *Problem:* Pupils often don't appreciate that the key function of the leaf is to make food for the plant. *Solution:* Revise the work covered in Unit 6A, Interdependence and Adaptation.
Sc3	**Properties of materials** *Problem:* Pupils think that all metals are magnetic (possibly a confusion with electrical conductivity). *Solution:* Recap on the work done in Activity 1 of Unit 6E, Forces in Action. Emphasise that only iron and steel are magnetic. **Thermal insulation** *Problem:* Pupils do not appreciate that thermal insulators will keep things cold: they associate insulation with keeping something warm or, incorrectly, with warming something up. *Solution:* Recap on the 'Which is the best insulator?' Activity in Unit 4C, Keeping Warm. Talk about 'keep cold' boxes and thermos flasks. (Pupil's Book 4, page 25)
Sc4	**Shadows** *Problem:* The pupils think that shadows are formed by 'reflection'. *Solution:* Recap Activity 1 in Unit 6F, How We See Things. In this context, contrast the blocking of light that occurs when a shadow is formed, with the reflection of light in mirrors. **Gravity** *Problem:* The origin of gravity being the force of attraction to the centre of the Earth is not well understood. *Solution:* Recap the work covered in Activity 2 in Unit 6E, Forces in Action. **The pitch and loudness of sounds** *Problem:* Pupils do not understand the difference between the pitch and loudness of a sound. *Solution:* Revisit some of the activities from the sound circus used in Unit 5F, Sound All Around. Emphasise that the pitch is concerned with how high or low a note is, not how loud it is.

Support Materials

Resource List: Early Years

Working Out of Doors

- access to a safe outdoor area
- a small named flag for each child
- small pieces of treasure
- plant containers
- potting compost
- plastic spoons or spades
- a watering jug
- white paper
- hand lenses
- straws
- paper, sticky tape, crayons, scissors
- plastic animals
- a sand tray or shallow trays
- small containers
- books about animals

Perishables
- small herb plants
- leaves
- salt dough
- leaf litter or similar
- sand, stones, wood, twigs, leaves

Book List
The Ladybird Hunt by Alison Norman, HarperCollins, ISBN 0 00 317 2422.

Looking at Ourselves

- a large plastic mirror
- paints and paper
- dressing-up clothes and accessories
- string
- a chair
- paper, glue and scissors
- paper bags or folded paper
- paper face shapes, paints, collage materials
- construction toys
- a timer
- a small suitcase or bag
- long card tubes or dowelling
- a collection of different gloves
- artefacts for a baby, a child and an adult
- sets of dressing-up clothes and artefacts

Perishables
- small pots containing 'smelly' materials
- small cards with a double-sided tape or glue covering
- dry but smelly materials, e.g. tea, herbs

Book List
Scarecrow's Secret by Heather Amery and Stephen Cartwright, Usborne, ISBN 0 7460 0584 9.

Seasonal Activities

- access to a safe outdoor area
- a watering can with a rose
- access to a tap
- a lamp or powerful torch
- a screen or pale wall
- puppets
- a mixing bowl and spoons
- small plastic containers
- string
- pictures of birds
- bubble mixture and blowers
- two washing-up bowls
- plastic animals
- towels

Perishables
- puddles!
- bird seed
- vegetable fat
- autumn leaves
- blocks of ice

Book List
Rafik's Icicle by Alison Norman, HarperCollins, ISBN 0 00 317 2422.

Making Special Places

- a dark area
- a variety of torches
- different materials for covering the torch ends including tissue paper
- a till and play money
- paper and wax crayons
- materials for junk modelling
- clean shoes and boots
- shoe boxes and a foot-measuring machine
- play materials to make a garden centre
- seed trays, plant containers
- labelled containers for storing 'junk' materials

Perishables
- seeds
- potting compost

Book List
Can't You Sleep Little Bear? by Martin Wardell and Barbara Firth, Walker Books, ISBN 0 7445 1316 2.
Acorn Games by Alison Norman, HarperCollins, ISBN 0 00 317 2422.
George's Wellingtons by Alison Norman, HarperCollins, ISBN 0 00 317 2422.

Resource List: Early Years

Sand Play
- sand trays or other suitable containers
- wet and dry sand
- small buckets, cups and containers
- jugs, watering cans
- scoops, spoons and plastic spades
- sand moulds
- sieves, colanders, funnels and containers with holes
- plastic animals and other toys
- wooden bricks
- water
- a selection of magnetic and non-magnetic objects
- marbles or small balls
- magnets taped to lolly sticks

Cooking and Food
- access to a hygienic area for food preparation
- cooking utensils
- an oven
- hand lenses
- clear plastic cups, spoons, plastic knives, bowls, paper plates, food wrap
- paper
- pictures of potatoes

Perishables
- different types of fruit
- flour, baking powder, margarine, an egg, brown sugar, bananas, milk
- fruit squash, drinking water
- a selection pack of breakfast cereals
- milk, water or fruit juice
- potatoes, butter
- bread rolls, margarine, toppings for bread roll faces

Book List
Handa's Surprise by Eileen Browne, Walker Books, ISBN 0 7445 3634 0.

Water Play
- a tray and small plastic bowls
- waterproof aprons
- spoons, spatulas, whisks
- jugs, funnels, watering cans, teapots, bottles and other containers – all made from plastic
- transparent plastic containers with lids
- droppers, syringes, plastic straws, sticks
- a variety of waterproof and absorbent materials, including shiny card pieces
- a collection of objects for squeezing and squirting water
- large plastic bottles
- food dye

Book List
The Wet Day by Alison Norman, HarperCollins, ISBN 0 00 317 2422.
An Evening At Alfie's by Shirley Hughes, Red Fox, ISBN 00 99 256045.

Art Activities
- powder paints
- paint pots, palates and other containers
- paint brushes, pieces of sponge
- droppers, straws
- spoons
- water
- paper, card
- glue, scissors, pencils
- collage materials
- rolling pins, pastry cutters
- translucent materials

Perishables
- dough

Resource List: Early Years

Sound and Listening

- commercially-produced and homemade instruments
- plastic film canisters
- a tray
- a sound lotto game
- a cassette recorder
- materials for filling 'shakers'
- five pairs of ready-made 'shakers'
- play telephones
- string telephones
- funnel telephones
- card tubes
- card 'ear trumpets'

Book List

We're Going On A Bear Hunt by Michael Rosen and Helen Oxenbury, Margaret McElderry Books, ISBN 0 7445 2323 0.

Lullabyhullaballo by Mick Inkpen, Hodder Children's Books, ISBN 0 340 62686 0.

Little Beaver And The Echo by Amy McDonald, Walker Books, ISBN 0 7445 2315 0.

Peace At Last by Jill Murphy, Macmillan Children's Books, ISBN 0 333 4185 6.

Toys and Games

- a collection of balls
- clear plastic two-litre bottles
- jugs and funnels
- toy vehicles
- a collection of toys that move in different ways
- string
- empty containers and other 'junk' materials
- card wheels
- Blu-tack
- a balloon pump, balloons
- magnets taped to lolly sticks
- magnetic and non-magnetic materials
- plastic film canisters
- shoebox lids
- paper, crayons, scissors
- paper plates
- a variety of different 'wind toys'
- paper
- access to a safe outdoor area

Perishables

- coloured water
- a helium balloon

Book List

Pushing Pumpkins by Alison Norman, HarperCollins. ISBN 0 00 317 2422.

The Blue Balloon by Mick Inkpen, Hodder and Stoughton, ISBN 0340 558 349.

Resource List: Year 1

Ourselves

- body-part words (on card)
- hand lenses
- a white cloth
- audio tape of familiar sounds
- a cassette recorder
- empty film canisters
- muslin or fine net curtain
- fruit pictures
- feely bags
- blindfolds
- magazines
- family photographs
- pictures of animals (young, adult)
- glue
- pictures of living and non-living things
- Post-it notes
- string

Perishables
- flower heads
- fruit samples (apple, lemon, orange, etc.)
- potato crisps (different flavours)
- tadpoles

Growing Plants

- pictures of commonly occurring plants
- Post-it notes
- a map of school grounds
- coloured pencils
- drawstring bag (feely bag)
- stones, soil, shredded paper, sand, concrete, sawdust
- teaspoons
- plant pots
- hand lenses
- plant part labels
- string

Perishables
- a selection of leaves
- dried bean mix
- a range of edible plants

Sorting and Using Materials

- objects made from metal, plastic, wood, paper, rock, glass
- feely bags, bar of soap, blindfolds
- samples of plastic, wood, metal, glass, fabric, stone, brick
- a fishing line with magnet attached
- cardboard fish with samples of material sellotaped to the back
- bar magnets
- wet and dry sand, clay, soil, gravel
- plastic trays
- lollipop sticks
- glue
- marbles
- clipboards
- pictures of house foundations
- samples of cotton, wool, sugar paper, newspaper, aluminium foil, plastic film
- yoghurt pots, teaspoons, syringes
- sand timers

Light and Dark

- a display of artefacts that either produce light or reflect it (mirrors, reflective strips, torches, metal spoons, lamps)
- Post-it notes
- a 'dark den' made from cardboard boxes or black sheeting
- cardboard boxes with a flap cut in one end and a circular hole in the top
- torches
- Compare bears or centi-cubes (different colours)
- squares of different materials, e.g. tissue paper, card, greaseproof paper, different fabrics, clear plastic, bubble wrap, sugar paper
- measuring tapes
- string

Resource List: Year 1

Pushes and Pulls

- a wooden/plastic building brick
- a toy car
- string
- objects that can be twisted or squeezed, e.g. sponge, rubber band
- a set of bar magnets
- a selection of toys to include: cars (simple push, wind-up or battery), baby cot toys, yoyo, water pistol, small sailing boat, balloon, party 'trumpets'
- a selection of balls of different masses and sizes that can be moved by blowing
- a hairdryer
- a tape measure
- a balance
- road safety information (posters, leaflets, videos)
- a copy of *The Green Cross Code*
- a 0.5 m ramp
- an assortment of toy cars
- masking tape

Sound and Hearing

- a large map of the school
- noise makers: rice in sealed plastic container, biscuit-tin drum, triangle, chime bar, elastic bands stretched round an open container, tubing (to spin around the head and make a whistle), whistle, recorder, bottles with various levels of water inside
- an audio tape of recorded sounds
- a cassette recorder
- instruments (including those from different cultures)
- name labels for instruments
- a ping-pong ball attached to a piece of cotton
- ear muffs
- drum sticks
- a blindfold
- an audio tape of music
- plastic cups
- various kinds of string
- clean empty cans (no sharp edges)

Resource List: Year 2

Health and Growth

- pictures of food and drink
- pictures of different types of meals
- pictures of people undertaking different types of activities
- a selection of pet food packaging
- a selection of medication packaging
- powders in sealed clear plastic bags, e.g. flour, semolina, corn flour, washing powder
- bowls
- different samples of soap
- different forms of 'dirt', e.g. soil, powder paint
- an ink pad

Plants and Animals in the Local Environment

- hand lenses
- paint
- life cycle pictures
- wildlife TV programmes
- mini-beast collecting apparatus, e.g. bug boxes, soft paint brushes, white sheets, specimen bottles
- sheet for mini-beast identification
- clip board

Perishables
- autumn fruits

Variation

- pictures of animals and plants
- hoops (for making groups)
- video clips of animals
- photographs of pupils and members of staff
- rulers
- measuring tapes

Perishables
- examples of plants

Grouping and Changing Materials

- a collection of materials: wood, metal, plastic, fabric, glass, rock (objects as well as pieces of the materials)
- raw wool and a woollen object
- cake mix
- salt and flour for making salt dough
- clay
- access to a kiln
- a candle (in sand tray) or hot plate
- aluminium foil containers
- tongs
- yoghurt pots
- a kettle
- a glass dish
- assorted rubber bands
- standard masses

Perishables
- chocolate
- butter or margarine
- ice cubes

Science Directions Co-ordinator's Handbook Photocopiable Master © HarperCollins*Publishers* Ltd 2001

Resource List: Year 2

Forces and Movement	Using Electricity
• plasticine • toys • pictures of toys • corks with holes down the centre • cocktail sticks • balsa wood • a syringe • a hairdryer or battery-powered fan • shoe boxes • knitting needles • bean bags or loaded shoes (to pull over surfaces) • newtonmeters (if appropriate) • bulldog buggies made from wheels, rulers, bulldog clips and dowel • plasticine • ramps • tape measures	• a range of cells of different sizes and voltages • magazines and catalogues • plastic-coated wires with the ends stripped • bulbs and bulb holders • masking tape • plastic-covered leads and crocodile clips • cells and cell holders • buzzers • aluminium fcil • split pins • paper clips • motors

Resource List: Year 3

Teeth and Eating	Helping Plants Grow Well
• clean, empty food packaging • pictures of pets • skulls of various animals • pictures of skulls • dental mirrors • a large drawing of teeth • samples of sterilised teeth • a tooth that has been soaked in a fizzy drink • hand lenses • a model tooth cut out of expanded polystyrene • nail varnish remover • a chicken bone • vinegar • old white tiles (surface scratched with sandpaper) • substances to use as stains, e.g. orange/blackcurrant juice, curry powder, tomato sauce, chocolate, tea, coffee • toothbrushes or cotton buds • a variety of toothpastes • bicarbonate of soda • timers	• pictures of a range of fruits and vegetables • modelling materials (for making fruits and vegetables) • a glass vase • food colouring • a knife • a ruler • empty film canisters • compost • plastic bottles • measuring cylinders or syringes • a thermometer • cardboard box • strips of cardboard • black plastic bags *Perishables* • a range of fruits and vegetables • plants in flower, e.g. geraniums • a bulb, e.g. tulip • celery • radish seeds • a bean plant

 Science Directions Co-ordinator's Handbook Photocopiable Master © HarperCollins*Publishers* Ltd 2001

Resource List: Year 3

Characteristics of Materials

- a wide range of materials including: wood, rock, iron/steel, paper, plastic (polythene), fabric
- a hammer
- bar magnets
- samples of floor covering: wood, carpet, plastic tiles, ceramic tiles
- a cardboard tube
- a heavy object such as a stone
- objects for 'rub' test: stone, brick, sandpaper
- different types of kitchen roll, paper towels or paper handkerchiefs
- saucers or plastic trays
- measuring cylinders or syringes
- small cardboard boxes
- a range of packaging materials: polystyrene pieces, bubble wrap, shredded paper, newspaper, fabric samples
- aluminium foil cases
- water bowls
- different samples of paper
- a hole punch
- yoghurt pots
- string
- 100 g masses

Perishables
- small meringue nests
- chocolate, butter, sugar and salt

Rocks and Soils

- rock samples: granite, limestone (chalk), marble, slate, sandstone
- a sample of coal
- a sample of wood
- samples of brick, concrete (breeze block), iron, plastic
- sand, clay and peat soils
- hand lenses
- sandpaper
- a dropping pipette
- large measuring cylinders or clear plastic beakers
- filter funnels
- measuring cylinders
- timers

Magnets and Springs

- plasticine
- an assortment of magnets: bar, horseshoe, circular
- magnetic games and fridge magnets
- paper clips
- an assortment of rubber bands
- an assortment of springs
- newtonmeters
- multilink cubes or small bricks
- tape measures

Light and Shadows

- torches
- an overhead projector
- a slide projector
- fabric samples
- coloured acetate (sweet wrappers)
- a white board or large sheet of paper
- a comb
- chalk
- a camera
- a figure (doll)
- 10 cm diameter paper circles
- a shadow stick (broom handle)
- greaseproof paper, Clingfilm, transparent coloured film
- a dowel

Resource List: Year 4

Moving and Growing
- a model skeleton
- a chicken leg bone
- an assortment of animal bones
- a knife
- pictures of animals with exoskeletons
- cardboard tubes of three different thicknesses
- split pins
- rubber bands
- measuring tapes
- callipers

Perishables
- a chicken leg

Habitats
- hoops for a sorting activity
- pond-dipping equipment
- hand lenses
- pooters
- bug boxes
- soft paint brushes
- sample bottles
- white trays
- a simple invertebrate key
- a simple tree key
- a suitable video on food chains
- newspaper cuttings on current environmental issues
- large jars
- gravel

Perishables
- pond life (snails)
- pond weed

Keeping Warm
- large bowls
- alcohol thermometers
- a range of other types of thermometer: forehead, soil, household (circular), temperature sensor/data logger and computer
- a printout from temperature sensor
- polystyrene cups and lids
- weather maps from newspapers
- city temperatures from newspapers
- a plan of the school
- access to an oven
- an insulated food box
- timers
- a range of materials: newspaper, fabric, kitchen roll, toilet paper
- ice boxes, insulated bags and canisters, drinks containers
- magazines
- a cooking pan with wooden or plastic handle
- a kettle
- an assortment of spoons: wooden, metal, plastic
- rubber bands
- a balance

Perishables
- soup
- an instant noodle meal
- jacket potatoes
- ice

Solids and Liquids
- a range of materials: wood, metal, glass, plastic, paper, card
- sand, salt, sugar (granular and lump), alum, flour, talcum powder, soil, chalk, pea shingle
- washing-up liquid
- tea bags
- coffee
- glasses or vases of different shapes
- a candle and sand tray
- small plastic trays or dishes
- thermometers
- stopwatches
- transparent plastic cups
- small spoons
- colanders and sieves
- filter funnels and filter paper
- yoghurt pots
- materials for use as filters: muslin, cotton wool, paper towels, aluminium foil, plastic foil
- coffee filters (bleached and unbleached)
- flat dishes or saucers
- measuring cylinders

Perishables
- lemonade
- cola
- tomato sauce

Resource List: Year 4

Friction

- margarine tubs
- an assortment of different masses
- newtonmeters
- rubber bands
- access to a bicycle
- shallow trays
- plasticine
- long transparent tubes or measuring cylinders
- cotton thread
- stopwatches
- parachute material (plastic or fabric)
- plastic figures (as parachutists)
- cake/bun cases

Perishables

- a range of lubricants: butter, margarine, tomato sauce, cooking oil

Circuits and Conductors

- a portable radio or CD player
- thin insulated wire
- plastic-covered leads and crocodile clips
- cells and holders
- bulbs and holders
- a range of metallic objects: scissors, beer bottle tops, nails, milk bottle tops, paper clips, tins, coins
- a range of non-metallic objects: cork, plastic carton, paper bag, wooden spoon, fabric
- motors
- buzzers
- LEDs
- aluminium foil
- split pins
- paper clips
- thick wire
- masking tape
- paper tissue

Resource List: Year 5

Keeping Healthy
- lifestyle magazines
  (e.g. *Healthy Living*)
- labels from food products
- a smoking machine (cotton wool,
  plastic piping, syringe, sticky tape,
  pin)
- assorted cigarettes (tipped, untipped,
  full-tar, low-tar)
- health education leaflets on drugs,
  alcohol, tobacco and exercise
- a model heart
- a scalpel
- a balloon pump
- a model or diagram of a torso
- stopwatches
- a video tape showing circulatory
  system and muscle movement
- pulse rate monitors (optional)
- limewater (optional)
- thermometers (LCD type)

Perishables
- a pig's heart
- a chicken leg

Life Cycles
- pictures of fruits: strawberry, orange,
  apple, coconut, tomato, pineapple,
  kiwi, mango
- a knife
- pictures of wind-dispersed seeds:
  barley, poppy, ash, sycamore, maize
- plastic petri dishes
- filter paper
- acetate grids
- a selection of fertilisers: Baby Bio,
  Phostrogen, plant food sticks
- a selection of pollutants: salt, washing
  powder, washing-up liquid
- plastic lemonade bottles
- hand lenses
- a microscope

Perishables
- fruits: strawberry, orange, apple,
  coconut, tomato, pineapple, kiwi,
  mango
- wind-dispersed seeds: poppy, ash,
  sycamore, maize
- selection of seeds: cress, radish,
  tomato
- flowers: daffodil, buttercup

Gases All Around
- a large plastic syringe
- a transparent plastic bowl
- sealed syringes full of air,
  water and sand
- sand
- soil
- marbles of different sizes
- jars or yoghurt pots, measuring
  cylinders
- an air freshener aerosol
- a range of insulating materials:
  cotton wool, expanded polystyrene,
  bubble wrap, shredded newspaper,
  fabrics
- drinks cans
- cut-off plastic lemonade bottles or
  plastic tubs
- thermometers
- timers
- kettles or an urn

Changing State
- candles in sand tray/holders or
  hot plate
- thermometers
- heat resistant containers: Pyrex
  dishes, metal pans
- a temperature sensor, data logger and
  computer (optional)
- saucers
- a transparent dome-shaped cover
- tin cans
- tongs
- fabric pieces (10 cm x 10 cm)
- a balance
- washing pegs
- a hairdryer or fan
- calculators

Perishables
- ice

Resource List: Year 5

Earth, Sun and Moon

- name cards for the planets
- a tape measure or trundle wheel
- a torch
- an overhead projector
- modelling clay
- a shadow stick (broom handle)
- a globe
- a football
- a tennis ball on a stick
- balloons
- a balloon pump
- drinking straws
- materials for balloon track: string, woollen thread, cotton thread, wire

Sounds All Around

- a metal rod
- a hammer
- a ball attached to a piece of string
- glass bottles
- a water jug
- plastic, wooden and metal rulers
- tuning forks
- cardboard tubes of different lengths
- a wooden board
- a block of wood
- a hammer and nails
- an old guitar or violin strings
- masses
- balloons
- a shiny metal tray
- a tape measure
- nails of different thicknesses
- dowelling
- art straws
- a range of musical instruments
- cardboard boxes
- a range of soundproofing materials: paper, foil, fabric, bubble wrap
- cells
- insulated wires and crocodile clips
- buzzers
- a tape measure

Resource List: Year 6

Interdependence and Adaptation
- leaf identification keys
- habitat guides and reference books
- hand lenses
- collecting tubes for invertebrates
- card and string
- hand lenses or binocular microscopes
- filter funnels
- measuring cylinders
- cotton wool
- plastic petri dishes
- netting (old fine net curtains)
- black paper

Perishables
- four pot plants
- soil samples (sandy, stony, clay)
- woodlice or blow fly larvae

Micro-organisms
- transparent containers
- hand lenses
- a balance
- syringes
- plastic beakers

Perishables
- samples of food
- flour
- yeast (fresh or dried)
- yeast/sugar solution
- cooking oil
- sugar

More About Dissolving
- sieves
- solids (sand, small shingle, wood chippings, rice, salt)
- sea salt crystals
- coffee filters
- filter paper
- funnels
- transparent plastic containers
- yoghurt pots/containers
- Pyrex containers (for heating ink)
- candles/night lights and holders
- blue ink
- black (washable) ink
- felt-tip pens
- salt solution
- mixture of salt, iron filings, marbles, sand, broken matchsticks, small stone chippings
- magnets
- tweezers
- stirrers or spoons
- plastic bags
- droppers
- stopwatches or timers
- a balance
- measuring cylinders
- thermometers
- a kettle or urn

Perishables
- granulated sugar
- sugar lumps
- icing sugar
- flour

Reversible and Irreversible Changes
- spoons
- salt
- measuring cylinders
- a kettle
- sand trays and candles or night lights and holders
- matches
- jam jars of different sizes
- measuring cylinders
- stopwatches
- tongs
- materials to burn: paper, wood shavings, fabric, string

Perishables
- effervescent tablets or powder (Aspro Clear, Andrews)

Science Directions Co-ordinator's Handbook Photocopiable Master © HarperCollins*Publishers* Ltd 2001

Resource List: Year 6

Forces in Action

- materials (plastic, wood, metal: aluminium, copper, iron/steel)
- bar magnets
- forcemeters/newtonmeters
- magazines
- scissors and glue
- rubber bands of different thicknesses
- rulers
- assorted masses (100 g, 500 g and 1 kg)
- small springs (optional)
- plastic beakers
- card for making spinners
- scissors
- paper clips
- stop watches
- cake/bun cases
- calculators

Perishables
- cooking oil

How We See Things

- a high-powered torch or overhead projector
- torches
- a large sheet of paper
- a cardboard comb
- lenses
- plane mirrors
- spoons
- convex and concave mirrors
- foil (aluminium and coloured)
- fabric
- plates
- cutlery
- perspex
- scissors
- bathroom tiles
- tape measures
- rulers
- card to make shapes

Changing Circuits

- plastic-covered leads
- crocodile clips
- cells and holders
- bulbs and holders
- switches or card and aluminium foil, or split pins and paper clips to make switches
- motors
- buzzers
- coloured tissue (red, amber, green)
- fuse wire or nichrome wire

Key Facts Sc2: Life Processes and Living Things

- Tobacco, alcohol and other drugs can have a harmful effect on the body.
- Some drugs are addictive.
- The heart acts as a pump.
- Exercise affects your heart rate.
- Exercise is needed in order to keep healthy.
- Blood circulates around the body through vessels (arteries, capillaries and veins).
- Exercise affects how fast the blood is pumped.
- Plants have different parts in order for them to make seeds and reproduce.
- Female parts of a flower are called carpels; they are made up of the stigma, style and ovary.
- Male parts of the flower are called stamens; they are made up of the anther and the filament.
- Plants need light, water, air and warmth in order to grow well.
- Pollination can take place in two ways: by the wind or insects.
- Male and female parts of a plant combine to form seeds.
- Seeds can be dispersed in a number of different ways, e.g. by animals or the wind.
- The leaves of green plants produce food in order for the plant to grow; this process is called photosynthesis.
- Water and minerals are taken in by the roots and transported to the leaves.
- Different plants and animals are found in different habitats.
- Animals and plants in different habitats are suited to the conditions there.
- Food chains show what eats what in a habitat.
- Nearly all food chains start with a green plant.
- Micro-organisms are too small to be seen.
- Some micro-organisms are harmful.
- Micro-organisms can be helpful.
- Yeast is an example of a helpful micro-organism.

Science Directions Co-ordinator's Handbook Photocopiable Master   © HarperCollins*Publishers* Ltd 2001

Key Facts Sc3: Materials and their Properties

- Materials have different properties, for example, hardness, flexibility, strength.

- Some materials like iron and steel are magnetic; other metals are not magnetic.

- Temperature is measured using thermometers.

- Objects cool or warm to the temperature of their surroundings.

- Materials that allow heat to pass through them quickly are called thermal conductors.

- Materials that do not allow heat to pass through them quickly are called thermal insulators.

- Many good insulators work because they trap air.

- Thermal insulators keep warm things warm and cold things cold.

- Electrical conductors let electricity pass through them.

- Electrical insulators stop electricity passing through them.

- All metals are electrical conductors.

- Materials can be classified as natural (e.g. wood) or manufactured (e.g. plastic).

- Soil is made from particles of rock.

- Common types of soil are clay soil, sandy soil and peat.

- The plant material in soil is called humus.

- Solids have a fixed shape; liquids and gases take the shape of the container they are in.

- Gases can be squashed or compressed; solids and liquids are not easily compressed.

Key Facts Sc3: Materials and their Properties

- Air is a mixture of gases.

- Oxygen is the gas that humans and animals need to stay alive.

- A solid dissolves when it is broken down by water into very small pieces.

- When a solid dissolves, it forms a solution.

- A solid that dissolves in a liquid is soluble.

- A solid that does not dissolve in a liquid is insoluble.

- The speed of dissolving can be increased by:
  breaking up the solid;
  stirring;
  heating the solution.

- Melting, boiling, condensing, freezing and evaporating are reversible changes.

- In the water cycle, water evaporates and forms water vapour; the water vapour then condenses to form clouds.

- In an irreversible change, a new substance is made.

- Burning is an example of an irreversible change.

- Sieving can be used to separate solid particles of different sizes.

- Filtering can be used to separate a solid from a liquid.

- Filtering will not remove the solid dissolved in a solution.

- Evaporation can be used to remove a liquid from a solution.

 Science Directions Co-ordinator's Handbook Photocopiable Master © HarperCollins*Publishers* Ltd 2001

Key Facts Sc4: Physical Processes

Electricity

- Electricity will only flow when there is a complete circuit.

- Electrical conductors (all metals) allow electricity to pass through them; electrical insulators do not.

- Switches are used to control the flow of electricity.

- The following components can be represented by symbols in an electrical circuit:

  cell;   bulb;   switch;   motor;   buzzer.

- The brightness of a bulb in a circuit can be changed by:

  changing the number of cells;

  changing the number of bulbs;

  changing the length of the wire in the circuit.

Forces

- Iron and steel are magnetic materials.

- The ends of a magnet are called the north pole and the south pole.

- Like magnetic poles repel each other; unlike magnetic poles attract each other.

- Force is measured in newtons using a newtonmeter.

- The direction of a force can be shown on drawings using an arrow.

- Gravity is a force that pulls things towards the ground.

- The force of gravity on the Moon is less than the force of gravity on the Earth.

- Friction is a force that stops things from moving.

- Lubricants are used to reduce friction and make things move easily.

- Air resistance and water resistance are both friction forces.

- Streamlining is used to reduce friction forces.

- When a spring is stretched, the stretching force is opposed by a reaction force.

Key Facts Sc4: Physical Processes

Light and Sound

- There are a number of different sources of light.

- Light travels from a source.

- Light cannot pass through some materials; when this happens, a shadow is formed.

- Light is reflected from surfaces.

- Images can be seen in a mirror.

- Sounds are made when objects vibrate.

- Sound needs a medium through which to travel.

- The pitch and loudness of a sound can be changed.

- The pitch of a sound describes how high or low the note is.

- Although sounds are made when objects vibrate, we cannot always see the vibrations.

The Earth and Beyond

- The Sun, Earth and Moon are spherical (the same shape as a football).

- The length and direction of shadows change during the day.

- The apparent movement of the Sun is due to the rotation of the Earth.

- It takes the Earth one year to make a complete orbit of the Sun.

- It takes the Earth 24 hours to make one complete rotation on its axis.

- Day and night occur because the Earth rotates on its axis.

- It takes the Moon 28 days to make one complete orbit of the Earth.

Science Directions Co-ordinator's Handbook Photocopiable Master   © HarperCollins*Publishers* Ltd 2001

Glossary of Terms

Sc2

addict
a person who has become dependent on something, e.g. drugs.

addictive
if a substance is addictive then it contains chemicals that make people want to keep taking it.

alcohol
the substance that is found in beer and drinks like whisky and is produced by microbes.

arteries
blood vessels that carry blood away from the heart.

bacteria
very small organisms that can cause disease in humans.

carnivore
a flesh-eating animal.

chlorophyll
the green substance found in leaves.

consumer
any organism that eats other organisms.

dependent
a person is said to be dependent when they suffer side effects if they do not continue to use a drug.

disease
an illness.

drug abuse
when drugs are taken without following instructions or in amounts larger than recommended.

fertilisation
the point at which the male part of a living thing meets and joins with the female part.

food chain
a diagram that shows what eats what.

germ
another word for bacteria.

habitat
an environment that contains its own particular organisms, e.g. a desert.

herbivore
an animal that eats plants.

Glossary of Terms

microbe
see micro-organism.

micro-organism
an organism that can only be seen using a microscope, e.g. bacteria.

nicotine
a substance contained in tobacco, which is addictive (see above).

optic nerve
the nerve that connects the back of the eye to the brain.

photosynthesis
a process that takes place in a leaf where the plant uses light, carbon dioxide and water to produce sugar.

pollination
the transfer of pollen grains from the stamens to the stigma.

pollution
damage to the environment by substances that harm living things.

preserve
to keep from being contaminated by micro-organisms.

producer
an organism that is able to produce its own food.

pulse rate
the number of times the pulse beats in one minute.

veins
blood vessels that carry blood from the body and back to the heart.

virus
a very small microbe that can cause disease.

Sc3

boiling point
the temperature at which a liquid changes into a gas or vapour.

carbon dioxide
one of the gases that make up the air.

condense
to change from a gas or vapour to a liquid. This happens when the gas or vapour is cooled down.

 Science Directions Co-ordinator's Handbook Photocopiable Master   © HarperCollins*Publishers* Ltd 2001

Glossary of Terms

dissolve
when a solid is broken into such small pieces by a liquid that the pieces cannot be seen.

distillation
the process where a liquid evaporates when it is heated and then condenses when it is cooled.

evaporation
the process where a liquid changes to a gas or vapour.

filtering
the process where a solid is separated from a liquid. The filter has small holes that the liquid can pass through but the solid cannot.

fire extinguisher
a device that contains a substance that will put out a fire.

freezing
the point at which a liquid changes into a solid (also called 'solidification').

fuel
a substance that burns and produces energy.

insoluble
describes a solid that does not dissolve in a liquid.

irreversible
a change that cannot be reversed, e.g. burning a candle.

melting
the point at which a solid changes into a liquid.

mineral
a substance which is taken out of the ground.

nitrogen
one of the gases that make up the air. Most of the air is nitrogen.

oxygen
one of the gases in the air. It is the gas that animals need to stay alive.

particles
small parts that make up any substance.

Glossary of Terms

reversible

if something is reversible it can be changed back. Melting is a reversible change – the liquid can be changed back into a solid by freezing.

solidification

the point at which a liquid changes into a solid (also called 'freezing').

soluble

describes a solid that dissolves in a liquid.

solution

the mixture formed when a solid dissolves in a liquid.

states of matter

there are three states of matter: solid, liquid and gas.

vapour

formed when a liquid evaporates, e.g. water vapour is formed when water evaporates.

water cycle

how water from rivers, lakes and the sea can form clouds, fall as rain and then return to where it came from.

Sc4

air resistance

a force that is caused by the air pushing against a moving object.

component

a device, like a bulb, or a buzzer, that is included in an electrical circuit.

compress

to make smaller by squashing or squeezing.

day

the time taken for a planet to spin once on its axis. The Earth takes 24 hours to spin once on its axis.

daytime

the time of day when a part of the Earth is facing the Sun and so receiving light from the Sun.

drag

a force that slows down a moving object. It is the same as air resistance or water resistance.

Earth

the planet that we live on.

Glossary of Terms

echo
a sound bouncing back from a solid surface.

electrical circuit
a selection of wires and components through which electricity can flow.

electrical current
a flow of electricity round a circuit. It is the current that makes a bulb light up or a buzzer buzz.

force
a push, pull, twist or squeeze.

friction
a force caused by two substances rubbing together.

gravity
a force that pulls all objects towards the centre of the Earth.

lens
a substance that focuses light so that an image can be seen.

Moon
a large object that orbits a planet. Our Moon orbits the Earth.

night
the time of day when a part of the Earth is facing away from the Sun and so receives no light.

noise pollution
when a noise becomes so loud that it can damage your hearing and becomes a nuisance to people who hear it.

orbit
the curved path of an object, e.g. the path the Earth takes around the Sun, or the Moon around the Earth.

parallel circuit
an electrical circuit which provides at least two routes for the electricity to flow through.

phases of the Moon
the changing shape of the Moon caused by different amounts of the Moon being lit up by the Sun.

Glossary of Terms

pitch

how high or low a note is.

planet

a large object that is found in a solar system. Unlike a Sun, a planet does not make its own light.

pupil

the black hole in the front of the eye that lets the light through.

reaction force

a force that acts against another force, e.g. when you stand on the ground, it provides a reaction force, which acts in the opposite direction to your weight.

reflect

to bounce off a surface.

retina

the layer of nerve cells at the back of the eye, which collects the images.

series circuit

an electrical circuit which allows only one route for the electricity to flow through.

Solar System

a group of planets orbiting or moving round a Sun. In our Solar System the Earth is one of nine planets which orbit the Sun.

source

the starting point for something.

streamlined

shaped so that air or water resistance is made as small as possible.

vibration

a movement backwards and forwards in quick succession.

year

the time taken for a planet to make one complete orbit of the Sun in its Solar System, e.g. the Earth takes 365 days, or one year, to orbit our Sun.

Science Directions Co-ordinator's Handbook Photocopiable Master   © HarperCollins*Publishers* Ltd 2001

Science Directions
Approaches to Assessment

Statutory Requirements

- National Curriculum levels must be used at the end of the key stage.

End-of-Year Summative Recording

- Unit-by-unit judgements aggregated to obtain an overall level for Sc1, 2, 3 and 4.

Unit-by-Unit Recording

- Significant activities chosen to provide evidence of typical attainment.

- Pupil responses matched against typical learning outcomes expressed in terms of levels.

- Pupil attainment recorded in terms of levels.

Work Scrutiny Recording Form

Nature of Work Sample:	Date:

Evidence of Pupil Attainment

Strengths	Development Points

Evidence of Effective Learning

Strengths	Development Points

Evidence of Effective Teaching

Strengths	Development Points

Science Directions Co-ordinator's Handbook Photocopiable Master   © HarperCollins*Publishers* Ltd 2001

Class Science Recording Sheet

Class

Teacher

Name	Previous Year					Unit A		Unit B		Unit C		Unit D		Unit E		Unit F		Unit G		End of Year				
	Sc1	Sc2	Sc3	Sc4	Sc all	Sc1 poc	Sc 234	Sc1 poc	Sc 234	Sc1 poc	Sc 234	Sc1 poc	Sc 234	Sc1 poc	Sc 234	Sc1 poc	Sc 234	Sc1 poc	Sc 234	Sc1	Sc2	Sc3	Sc4	Sc all

Note for Sc1: planning (p); obtaining and presenting evidence (o); considering evidence and evaluating (c).

Model: Short-term Plan for Science

Date 01.04.01   **Time**   Tuesday 1.30pm. 1.5 hrs

Objectives	Activities
From Science Directions Teaching File 2, page 41, Forces and Movement ● Pupils will be able to describe how wind and water can produce a force. **Resources** As page 41, Pupil Book pages 34 and 35	Together, all pupils will discuss water-mills and windmills and will be questioned about how they work. Establish that it is the force of the wind or water that makes them move. Show them the resources and challenge them to make a waterwheel or a windmill. Pupils to work in pairs – not George and Joe together. Green and red table to make windmills. Mrs Brown, the TA, will work with blue table on water wheels. Yellow table also to make water wheels. Ask the pupils how they could test the effectiveness of their wheels. Each group to demonstrate how they work and talk about the forces that they are using. **Plenary** Use the Pupil Book to answer questions about the force of water.

Science Directions Co-ordinator's Handbook Photocopiable Master   © HarperCollins*Publishers* Ltd 2001

Theme: Life Processes and Living Things (Sc2)

Unit	Activity	Key Concepts							
		Life Processes	Human and Other Animals			Plants		Variation	Ecology (Habitats)
			Nutrition/ Circulation	Movement/ Growth	Health	Plant Growth	Plant Reproduction		
EY Working out of Doors	Special Places							•	•
	Treasure Hunt							•	•
	A Pot of Plants						•		
	Looking for Leaves								
	Small Animal Search			•				•	•
	Making Habitats		•	•	•				•
EY Seasonal Activities	Feeding the Birds	•	•	•					•
	Autumn Faces			•					
EY Looking at Ourselves	Looking in the Mirror	•			•		•		
	Scarecrows		•	•	•				
	Hairy Puppets							•	
	Hand Built			•	•				
	Smelly Cards	•		•	•				
	I Packed My Bag	•		•	•				
EY Making Special Places	The Garden Centre					•		•	
EY Cooking and Food	Fruit Salad	•	•	•	•				
	A Big Breakfast		•	•	•				
1A Ourselves	1 Body Parts	•	•						
	2 Sensory Carousel	•							
	3 Looking at Change	•		•				•	
	4 Comparing Adults and Young		•	•	•			•	
	5 Movement Classification	•						•	
	6 Are the Oldest Children the Tallest?	•		•	•			•	

Theme: Life Processes and Living Things (Sc2)

Unit	Activity	Life Processes	Nutrition/ Circulation	Movement/ Growth	Health	Plant Growth	Plant Reproduction	Variation	Ecology (Habitats)
			Human and Other Animals			**Plants**			
1B Growing Plants	1 What is a Plant?	•				•			
	2 Plant Part Identification Walk	•				•			
	3 Bean Sorting	•				•	•		
	4 Investigating Plant Growth	•				•			
	5 Roots, Shoots and Edible Parts				•	•			
	6 Plant Growth Investigation	•				•			
2A Health and Growth	1 Food Sort	•	•						
	2 Favourite Food Survey	•	•						
	3 Making Comparisons of Meals	•	•						
	4 What Do Pets Eat?	•	•						
	5 The Safe Use of Medicines	•			•				
	6 How Clean Are Your Hands?	•			•				
2B Plants and Animals in the Local Environment	1 Sorting Animals and Plants	•						•	
	2 Local Habitat Survey								•
	3 Autumn Seed Collection								•
	4 Animal Life Cycles	•		•					•
	5 Sorting Mini-beasts	•							•
	6 Exploring Mini-beasts	•							•
2C Variation	1 Animal and Plant Characteristic Quiz	•							•
	2 Similar Features	•						•	•
	3 Description of a Friend							•	•
	4 Local Resident Survey							•	•
	5 Common Plant Parts					•			
	6 Measuring Hand Spans and Feet							•	

Key Concepts

Theme: Life Processes and Living Things (Sc2)

Unit	Activity	Life Processes	Nutrition/ Circulation	Movement/ Growth	Health	Plant Growth	Plant Reproduction	Variation	Ecology (Habitats)
			Human and Other Animals			Plants			
3A Teeth and Eating	1 Supermarket Survey		•						
	2 Diet Does Not Mean Thin	•	•						
	3 Pet-food Survey	•	•						
	4 Teeth				•				
	5 Healthy Gums				•				
	6 How Clean Are Your Teeth?				•				
3B Helping Plants Grow Well	1 Virtual Greengrocers	•				•			
	2 The Structure of Plants	•				•			
	3 The Root as a Special Organ	•				•			
	4 Greenhouse Investigation	•				•			
	5 Keeping Plants in the Dark	•				•			
	6 Greenhouse Investigation Conclusion	•				•			
4A Moving and Growing	1 Bone Location	•		•					
	2 Parts of the Human Skeleton	•		•					
	3 Skeletons of Other Animals	•		•					
	4 Muscles			•					
	5 Animals Without Skeletons	•		•					
	6 Do People With the Longest Legs Jump the Furthest or the Highest?			•				•	•
4B Habitats	1 Picture Sort							•	•
	2 School Grounds Survey							•	•
	3 Invertebrate Survey	•						•	•
	4 Food Chains	•							•
	5 Protection of the Environment								•
	6 Habitat Help								•

Key Concepts

Theme: Life Processes and Living Things (Sc2)

Unit	Activity	Life Processes	Human and Other Animals			Plants		Variation	Ecology (Habitats)
			Nutrition/ Circulation	Movement/ Growth	Health	Plant Growth	Plant Reproduction		
5A Keeping Healthy	1 What is Health?	•		•					
	2 Food Groups	•	•	•					
	3 Drugs and Smoking	•	•						
	4 Blood and Circulation			•					
	5 Muscles and Movement				•				
	6 Energy and Exercise			•					
5B Life Cycles	1 Sequencing Plant Life Cycles	•					•		
	2 Seed Dispersal	•				•	•		
	3 Investigating the Germination and Growth of Seedlings	•				•			
	4 Insect Pollination	•		•					
	5 Human Reproduction	•					•		
	6 Seedlings Revisited					•			
6A Interdependence and Adaptation	1 The Needs of Plants Revisited	•				•			
	2 Habitat Visit								•
	3 Food Chains		•						•
	4 Different Habitats								•
	5 Soils From Different Habitats		•						•
	6 What do Mini-beasts Prefer?								•
6B Micro-organisms	1 What Makes us Ill?				•				
	2 Jenner Revisited				•				
	3 Mouldy Food	•							
	4 Yeast	•							

(Key Concepts)

Theme: Grouping and Classifying Materials (Sc3)

Unit	Activity	Key Concepts				
		Common Materials/ Simple Properties	Natural/ non-natural	Property to Use	Rocks and Soils	Solids, Liquids and Gases
EY Seasonal Activities	Muddy Puddles	●				●
	Ice Cold Animals	●				●
EY Making Special Places	The Shoe Shop	●				
	The Recycling Centre	●				
EY Sand Play	Burrowing	●				
	Buried Treasure	●				
EY Water Play	Drip Drop	●				
	Fill It Up	●				●
	Putting Them in Water	●				
EY Art Activities	Sticking Pictures	●				
	Making Coloured Windows	●				
1C Sorting and Using Materials	1 Describing Objects	●				
	2 Matching Materials	●				
	3 Using Magnets	●				
	4 Materials for a Specific Use	●		●		
	5 Best Builder	●		●		
	6 Which is the Best Material to Use for an Umbrella?			●		
2D Grouping and Changing Materials	1 Sorting Materials	●				
	2 Natural Materials		●			
	6 Which is the Most Stretchy Rubber Band?	●				

Theme: Grouping and Classifying Materials (Sc3)

Unit	Activity	Key Concepts				
		Common Materials/ Simple Properties	Natural/ non-natural	Property to Use	Rocks and Soils	Solids, Liquids and Gases
3C Characteristics of Materials	1 Classifying Materials	•		•		
	2 Which is the Hardest Material?	•		•		
	3 Which is the Best Paper Towel?	•		•		
	4 Which is the Best Packaging Material?	•		•		
	6 Which is the Strongest Paper to Use for Paper Bags?	•		•		
3D Rocks and Soils	1 Rocks as Natural Materials	•	•		•	
	2 Examining Rocks	•			•	
	3 Comparing the Hardness and Permeability of Rocks	•			•	
	4 Research into Different Types of Rock	•			•	
	5 Looking at Types of Soil	•			•	
	6 Comparing the Permeability of Different Types of Soil	•			•	
4C Keeping Warm	3 Keeping Things Hot	•		•		
	4 Thermal Insulators	•		•		
	5 Which is the Best Insulator?	•		•		
4D Solids and Liquids	1 Classifying Materials	•				•
5C Gases All Around	1 Solids, Liquids and Gases	•				•
	2 Comparing the Air Content of Different Soils	•			•	•
	4 Common Gases	•				•
	5 Investigating Insulators	•		•		•

Theme: Changing Materials (Sc3)

Unit	Activity	Key Concepts				
		Heating Materials	Mixing Materials	Temperature	Reversible Changes	Non-reversible Changes
EY Seasonal Activities	Ice Cold Animals	•				
EY Cooking and Food	Banana Bread	•	•			
	Fruity Drinks		•			
	A Big Breakfast	•	•			
	One Potato, Two Potato	•				
EY Art Activities	Mixing and Painting		•			
	Drippy Pictures		•			
2D Grouping and Changing Materials	3 Heating Materials (1)	•				
	4 Heating Materials (2)	•				
	5 Melting Ice	•			•	
3C Characteristics of Materials	5 Which Substances Melt?	•			•	
4C Keeping Warm	1 Temperature			•		
	2 Measuring Temperature Around the School			•		
4D Solids and Liquids	2 Changing Solids to Liquids	•			•	
	3 Adding Solids to Water: Dissolving		•		•	
	6 Investigating Dissolving		•		•	
5C Gases All Around	3 Evaporation	•			•	
5D Changing State	1 States of Matter and Processes				•	
	2 Changing Ice	•			•	
	3 The Water Cycle	•			•	
	6 How Air Flow Affects Evaporation				•	
6C More About Dissolving	5 Factors Affecting Dissolving		•		•	
	6 How Temperature Affects How Quickly Sugar Dissolves		•		•	
6D Reversible and Irreversible Changes	1 Classifying Changes				•	•
	2 Burning as an Irreversible Change					•
	3 What Factors Affect the Burning of a Candle?					•

Theme: Separating Mixtures (Sc3)

Unit	Activity	Key Concepts		
		Sieving	Filtering	Evaporation
4D Solids and Liquids	4 Which is the Best Filter?		●	
	5 Separating the Mixture	●	●	
5D Changing State	4 Obtaining Pure Water			●
	5 Purifying Water		●	
6C More About Dissolving	1 Dissolving		●	
	2 Evaporation			●
	3 Separating Mixtures	●	●	
	4 Chromatography		●	

Theme: Electricity (Sc4)

Unit	Activity	Everyday Use	Simple Series Circuits	Key Concepts Using Switches	Changing Components	Circuit Diagrams
EY Toys and Games	Toys That Move	•				
2F Using Electricity	1 Electricity All Around	•				
	2 Simple Circuits (1)	•	•			
	3 Simple Circuits (2)	•	•			
	4 Making a Switch	•		•		
	5 Make a Picture of a Clown	•		•		
4F Circuits and Conductors	1 Electrical Circuits	•	•		•	
	2 Conductors and Insulators	•	•			
	3 Switches	•	•	•	•	
	4 Making Use of Electricity	•	•	•		
	5 What Affects the Brightness of a Bulb?	•	•	•	•	
6G Changing Circuits	1 Circuits and Circuit Diagrams	•	•	•		•
	2 Solving the 'Traffic Light' Problem	•	•	•		•
	3 How Does the Length of Wire in a Circuit Affect the Brightness of a Bulb?	•	•	•	•	•

Theme: Forces (Sc4)

Unit	Activity	Magnetism	Pushes/Pulls and Movement	Friction	Gravity	Measuring Forces	Direction of Forces	Opposing Forces
				Key Concepts				
EY Seasonal Activities	Streamers and Bubbles		•					
EY Sand Play	Buried Treasure	•						
	Helter-Skelter		•					
EY Water Play	Squeezing and Squirting		•					
EY Toys and Games	Toys That Move		•					
	Rolling Along		•					
	A Magnet Show	•	•					
	Up in the Air		•					
1E Pushes and Pulls	1 Making Things Move	•	•					
	2 Moving Toys		•					
	3 Blow Football		•					
	4 Forces and Safety		•					
	5 Which Car Will Travel the Furthest?		•					
2E Forces and Movement	1 Pushing and Pulling		•					
	2 Using the Wind and Water		•					
	3 Making a Wind Speed Measurer		•					
	4 How Slippery is the Floor?		•	•				
	5 Bulldog Buggies		•	•	•			
3E Magnets and Springs	1 Forces		•		•			
	2 Magnets and Magnetic Materials	•	•					
	3 Which is the Strongest Magnet?	•	•					
	4 Stretching Springs and Rubber Bands		•		•	•		
	5 Investigating Catapults		•					

Theme: Forces (Sc4)

Unit	Activity	Key Concepts						
		Magnetism	Pushes/Pulls and Movement	Friction	Gravity	Measuring Forces	Direction of Forces	Opposing Forces
4E Friction	1 Forces All Around		•	•	•	•		
	2 Measuring Forces		•	•		•		
	3 Reducing Friction		•	•		•		
	4 Streamlining		•	•	•	•	•	
	5 Parachutes		•	•	•		•	
	6 Which Shoes Give the Best Grip?		•	•		•		
6E Forces in Action	1 Forces All Around	•	•		•	•	•	
	2 Gravity		•		•			
	3 Stretching a Rubber Band		•		•	•	•	•
	4 Weighing Objects in Air and Water		•		•	•	•	•
	5 Investigating Spinners		•	•	•		•	•

Theme: Light and Sound (Sc4)

Unit	Activity	Key Concepts				
		Light Sources	Effects of Light	Seeing	Making Sounds	Vibrations
EY Seasonal Activities	Shadow Play	●	●			
EY Making Special Places	In the Dark Cave	●				
EY Art Activities	Making Coloured Windows		●			
EY Sound and Listening	Making Sounds				●	
	Making Shakers				●	
	Musical Kim's Game				●	
	The Echo				●	
	A Listening Walk				●	
	Telephones				●	
1D Light and Dark	1 What is Light?	●				
	2 Dark Dens		●			
	3 The Black Box		●			
	4 What Lets Light Through?		●			
1F Sound and Hearing	1 Listening Walk				●	
	2 Sorting Instruments				●	
	3 Describing Sounds				●	●
	4 Instrument Data Search				●	
	5 Loud and Quiet				●	
	6 Moving Messages				●	

Science Directions Co-ordinator's Handbook Photocopiable Master © HarperCollins*Publishers* Ltd 2001

Theme: Light and Sound (Sc4)

Unit	Activity	Key Concepts				
		Light Sources	Effects of Light	Seeing	Making Sounds	Vibrations
3F Light and Shadows	1 Light and Dark Concepts	•	•	•		
	2 Shadow Formation	•	•			
	3 Body Shadows		•			
	4 Sun Movement		•			
	5 Shadows in the Classroom		•			
	6 Transparency Investigation	•	•			
5F Sound All Around	1 Sound Review				•	
	2 Sound Circus				•	•
	5 Musical Instruments				•	•
	6 Soundproofing				•	•
6F How We See Things	1 Shadows		•	•		
	2 Reflections		•			
	3 Reflecting Light		•			
	4 Investigating the Size of Shadows		•	•		

Theme: The Earth and Beyond (Sc4)

Unit	Activity	Key Concepts			
		Shadows/Apparent Movement of the Sun	Spherical Nature	Day and Night	Orbits
EY Seasonal Activities	Shadow Play	•			
3F Light and Shadows	4 Sun Movement	•			
5E Earth, Sun and Moon	1 Stars and Planets	•		•	•
	2 The Universe		•		
	3 Shadows	•			
	4 Day and Night			•	•
	5 The Moon				•

Science Directions Co-ordinator's Handbook Photocopiable Master   © HarperCollins*Publishers* Ltd 2001